Colonial
NORTH CAROLINA

JOE A. MOBLEY

THE
History
PRESS

Published by The History Press
Charleston, SC
www.historypress.com

First published 2023

Manufactured in the United States

ISBN 9781467151283

Library of Congress Control Number: 2022951598

CONTENTS

PREFACE

The history of any nation, state, colony or community is always complex. A historian who attempts to write such an account has to select, shape and simplify the source material. The history of colonial North Carolina defies simplification, and to recount that saga in one brief volume creates challenges. It would require a lifetime to relate all there is to know about early North Carolina. Nevertheless, this book intends to provide the reader with a concise and clear vision of the major political, social and economic elements that shaped North Carolina in the years prior to the American Revolution and its founding as a state.

In some ways, North Carolina's early history is unique in the American experience. Its peculiar coastal geography, for example, in large measure limited its place and success in a worldwide economy. The size of its intercolonial and international commerce was hindered by its Outer Banks and shallow sounds and inlets that deny it deepwater harbors. Most of its many immigrants arrived from other colonies, such as Virginia and Pennsylvania, rather than directly from overseas. Some historians have theorized that those circumstances made North Carolina "relatively disconnected," a remote backwater cut off from what they term the Atlantic World.*

The history of colonial North Carolina, however, should not be viewed as if the colony were an isolated place, existing only unto itself. North

---

* A recent discussion of colonial North Carolina's relationship with the so-called Atlantic World can be found in Bradford J. Wood's "A Colony Lost: North Carolina in Atlantic World Histories," *North Carolina Historical Review* 98 (April 2021): 123–51 (quotation on 128).

Carolina's story started before Europeans arrived, when its first inhabitants, the American Indians, dominated its forests and waterways. As Europe emerged from the Renaissance in the sixteenth century and began to seek new conquests in a new world unfolding on the western horizon, the land that would one day become North Carolina emerged as one of the earliest sites for discovery, exploration and settlement in America.

Despite North Carolina's limitations for maritime commerce due to its coastline, Britain and Europe relied on the colony for resources, as it was the largest export reservoir of naval stores in all the British colonies. These naval stores were the tar, pitch, turpentine and rosin produced from the sap of the longleaf pine trees that grew so abundantly in the colony. The Atlantic World's fleets of wooden ships, the mainstay of its international commerce, depended on those products for caulking, painting and the preservation of wood and rope. Other products of forest and field—such as lumber, tobacco, corn, pork and wheat—were also much in demand and tied North Carolina to the world economy.

It is true that most of North Carolina's immigrants came overland rather than through its coastal ports. But when they arrived, they did not come completely reborn. They were still very much English, Scottish, Swiss, German, French or Welsh and retained age-old customs and cultures that brought diverse and international elements into their new home. Certainly, no matter how enslaved Africans entered North Carolina—overland or by sea—the yoke of American slavery, born on the west coast of Africa and transported to America as part of the maritime commerce of the Atlantic World, left an indelible stain on the colony and its future. Slavery helped bind North Carolina to the other slaveholding colonies, such as its neighbors Virginia and South Carolina, and contributed to the profits of the international slave trade.

Throughout the colonial era, the ongoing political, economic and religious changes and turmoil—including revolts and wars—occurring in Europe and Britain always impacted, to one degree or another, the lives of Carolinians. To study the history of colonial North Carolina is, therefore, to study its place in the wider world of which it was a part. This book strives to emphasize that point.

The first European explorers to arrive in North Carolina came on missions for France and Spain. But those countries did not found permanent settlements. It would remain for Britain to settle, govern, regulate trade and retain the loyalty of North Carolina and the other British colonies prior to the outbreak of the American Revolution. Until that fateful revolt, the colony remained a child of the mother country across the Atlantic.

I offer this short book as an introduction to the history of colonial North Carolina for a general readership, especially students and newcomers to the state. Many books and articles about the colonial era have been written by some of the state's most prominent historians. Several of these scholars are quoted in the pages that follow, and a number of the works that have influenced this project are included in the bibliography at the end of this volume.

ACKNOWLEDGEMENTS

I wish to express my appreciation to several persons and agencies for their assistance in the production of this book. At the State Archives of North Carolina, Vann Evans, audiovisual materials archivist, provided many illustrations, and William H. Brown, registrar, cleared permission to use the photographs. I'd like to thank the North Carolina Office of Archives and History of the Department of Natural and Cultural Resources for its authorization to reproduce the maps by Mark A. Moore. Joseph A. Beatty and the staff of the Historical Research Office of the North Carolina Office of Archives and History offered helpful advice and encouragement. The images of Indians from the engravings of Theodor de Bry and the art of John White were made available online by the North Carolina Collection, Wilson Library, University of North Carolina at Chapel Hill. Most of all, I am grateful to my wife, Kathleen B. Wyche, for taking time to edit and proofread this volume for publication.

.

1

GEOGRAPHY AND NATIVE INHABITANTS

North Carolina's long and unique history began even before the first Europeans gazed upon its shores in the sixteenth century. As much as any factor, geography determined the early growth and development of the region that one day would be called North Carolina. It consists of three distinct geographical areas: the coastal plain, the Piedmont and the mountains.

The coastal plain extends inward from the Atlantic Ocean, rising from sea level to about five hundred feet in elevation. Its soil is black loam in some places and sandy in others, and the easternmost portion, which covers the area about 20 to 30 miles inland, is known as the tidewater. Just off the coast lie the Outer Banks, a unique string of sand islands that extend 175 miles southward from the Virginia border past Cape Hatteras to Cape Lookout. From that point, the North Carolina coastline continues all the way to Cape Fear and the state's southeast border with South Carolina. Between the Outer Banks and the mainland are a number of shallow sounds, of which Albemarle and Pamlico Sounds are the largest. Narrow inlets allow limited passage through the banks to the Atlantic Ocean.

The Piedmont begins and the coastal plain ends at the fall line, an irregular line formed by waterfalls and rapids on the rivers. The Piedmont plateau has a soil of stiff clay and rock and reaches westward to an altitude of 1,500 feet, where the mountains begin, eventually reaching a height of 6,684 feet. The three North Carolina mountain ranges are the Blue Ridge Mountains, the Great Smoky Mountains and the less extensive Black Mountains. They are part of the Appalachian chain, which extends from Alabama to northern Maine. Located in the Black Mountains, Mount Mitchell is the highest point in the United States east of the Mississippi River.

North Carolina has numerous rivers that flow in various directions. Those that pass through the coastal plain—such as the Chowan, the Roanoke, the Tar-Pamlico and the Neuse Rivers—drain into the sounds, where they are blocked from the Atlantic by the Outer Banks, which keeps the sounds shallow with sand and silt. Only the Cape Fear River enters directly into the ocean, but its outlet is made hazardous by Frying Pan Shoals. A number of rivers—the Yadkin–Pee Dee, the Broad and the Catawba Rivers, for example—meander out of the Piedmont into South Carolina. In the mountains, some rivers—like the French Broad, the Little Tennessee and the Watauga Rivers—travel westward into Tennessee. The New River, formed millions of years ago in the northwest corner of North Carolina, actually flows northward into Virginia and West Virginia. (In 1976, the New River was designated a National Scenic River and is now also a state park.)

It was North Carolina's coastal geography that, most of all, consigned the colony to a weak economy and slow social and cultural development as immigrants from overseas attempted to settle the region in the seventeenth and eighteenth centuries. The Outer Banks virtually landlocked the colony by forming the shallow sounds, narrow inlets and dangerous, storm-ridden capes that denied North Carolina the deepwater harbors that were so essential for a large, thriving maritime commerce. The Cape Fear area had a direct outlet to the Atlantic, but any port established there would always be hampered by the treacherous Frying Pan Shoals.

Although coastal trade was an important part of colonial North Carolina's commercial economy, because of the precarious topography of the coast, it never developed on the scale enjoyed by its neighbors Virginia and South Carolina, which had the advantage of deepwater export and import shipping. Other factors that contributed to the slow progress of "Poor Carolina" were a limited land transportation system, the absence of a large and profitable staple crop and shortages of labor and hard currency. Historian A. Roger Ekirch writes, "By the close of the colonial period, North Carolina's economy was more expansive and prosperous than it had been in earlier years....Yet the economy was still underdeveloped....Progress had been achieved during the eighteenth century, but economic prospects remained checkered."

Because of its sluggish early development, colonial North Carolina was often the victim of disparaging remarks by outsiders, such as the wealthy planter William Byrd of Virginia. In the early eighteenth century, Byrd portrayed North Carolina, which he condescendingly called "Lubberland," as a primitive place inhabited by uncivilized and lazy people. What work was accomplished, he maintained, was performed by women. He declared:

> The Men, for their Parts, just like the Indians, impose all the Work upon the poor Women. They make their Wives rise out of their Beds early in the Morning, at the same time they lye and Snore, till the Sun has run one third of his course, and disperst all the unwholesome Damps. Then, after Stretching and Yawning for half an Hour, they light their Pipes, and, under the Protection of a cloud of Smoak, venture out into the open Air; tho', if it happens to be never so little cold, they quickly return Shivering into the Chimney corner. When the weather is mild, they stand leaning with both their arms upon the corn-field fence, and gravely consider whether they had best go and take a Small Heat at the Hough: but generally find reasons to put it off till another time.
>
> Thus they loiter away their Lives, like Solomon's Sluggard, with their Arms across, and at the Winding up of the Year Scarcely have Bread to eat.
>
> To speak the Truth, tis a thorough Aversion to Labor that makes People file off to N Carolina, where Plenty and a Warm Sun confirm them in their Disposition to Laziness for their whole Lives.

George Burrington, a colonial governor of North Carolina much disliked by the population, echoed Byrd's opinion of the enterprise and motivation of colonial North Carolinians. He reported to the British government in 1731 that they "are not industrious."

On the eve of the American Revolution, Janet Schaw, a Scottish traveler and diarist who considered herself a "woman of breeding," said of North Carolinians, "Nature holds out to them everything that can contribute to conveniency, or tempt to luxury, yet the inhabitants resist both and if they can raise as much corn and pork, as to subsist them in the most slovenly manner, they ask no more; and as a very small proportion of their time serves for that purpose, the rest is spent in sauntering thro' the woods with a gun or sitting under a rustick shade, drinking New England rum made into a grog, the most shocking liquor you can imagine." Schaw confessed, however, that "these I speak of are only the peasantry of this country, as hitherto I have seen nothing else, but I make no doubt when I come to see the better sort, they will be far from this description."

Indeed, a visitor to North Carolina today would have only to view some of its colonial towns to grasp how exaggerated Byrd's and other critics' portraits of its English and European settlers were. Indicative of the enterprise,

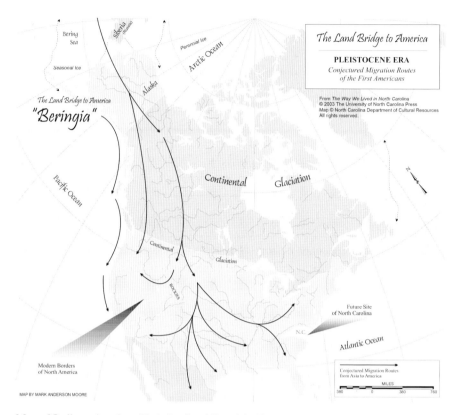

Map of Indian migration. *North Carolina Office of Archives and History.*

prosperity and sophistication of colonial Carolinians are such urban centers as Edenton, New Bern, Wilmington and Salem, as well as structures and sites throughout the countryside. Nevertheless, North Carolina's coastal trade limitations, poor land transportation and other difficulties did impede its economic and social development well into the nineteenth century.

But unlike the White immigrants when they arrived, North Carolina's first inhabitants, the American Natives, were not hindered in their lives and culture by limitations imposed by poor coastal navigation and other impediments to European-style progress. Over thousands of years, they had adapted to their environment without any major compulsion to alter it.

The ancestors of American Natives were Asians who migrated from Siberia over the Bering Strait Land Bridge into Alaska during the last ice age, perhaps as early as twenty-eight thousand years ago. From Alaska, they spread throughout the Americas, reaching North Carolina sometime around 10,000 BCE.

At that time, the first known Native culture, the Paleo culture, prevailed. This stone age way of life comprised nomadic hunters who followed herds of large animals, such as mammoths, bison and camels. The Paleo-Natives made tools and spear points from stone, and their major weapon was the spear, with which small bands of hunters killed their prey.

Around 8,000 BCE, the Archaic culture supplanted the Paleo tradition. The Archaic people were less nomadic than their predecessors and hunted smaller game as the larger animals died out. They developed the atlatl, a spear-throwing device that made hunting more efficient. They also became gatherers of plants, nuts, roots and fruit and carved crude pottery from soapstone.

By 1,000 BCE, the Woodland culture was replacing the Archaic. The Woodland folk cleared land and began growing crops, building permanent villages and making clay pottery. They developed the bow and arrow for hunting. The Woodland culture prevailed when Europeans arrived in North Carolina.

The new White immigrants also encountered the Mississippian culture. This culture developed around 700 CE in the vicinity of the Mississippi River and its connecting streams. The Mississippians were more reliant on agriculture than were the Woodland folk and had a more unified and organized political structure, which, at times, gained them military dominance over the Woodland people. They settled in villages protected by wooden palisades. They also constructed sophisticated ceremonial centers that featured large earthen mounds on which they built temples for conducting various ceremonies based on the cycles of nature and the growing and harvesting of crops, and they cleared nearby land for agriculture and for public games, dances and rituals.

Because Indians had no method of recording their daily lives through writing, much of what has been learned about them comes from archaeologists, who estimate that between fifty thousand and one hundred thousand Natives were living in North Carolina when Europeans first encountered them in the sixteenth century. At that point, the written historical record begins. About thirty tribes existed then, and they ranged from the coast to the mountains. The size of these tribes varied from a few hundred to several thousand people. The three largest tribes were the Tuscarora (coastal plain), the Catawba (Piedmont) and the Cherokee (mountains). All of these tribes belonged to one of three language groups: Algonquian, Iroquoian or Siouan. Tribes belonging to the same language group did not necessarily understand each other, in much the same way that, say, the French and Spanish do not speak the same language, even

North Carolina Indians in the sixteenth century. They often painted their bodies. *Engraving by Theodor de Bry from a painting by John White, North Carolina Collection, Wilson Library, University of North Carolina at Chapel Hill.*

though their languages have a common origin in Latin. One tribe might communicate with another through sign language or by speaking Mobilian, a type of common speech derived from the Choctaw tribe.

Native Carolinians established their villages near rivers and streams. They constructed their houses and lodges on a framework of bent limbs and saplings covered with bark, woven branches and skins. Subjected to the cold mountain climate, the Cherokee built earthen lodges. Household items within the dwellings included clay pottery, straw or cane mats and wooden benches and tools. Most villages had a council house for holding ceremonies and making governmental decisions. Sweat lodges made of earth also served the community.

All the tribes subsisted by hunting, fishing, gathering and farming. They hunted with bows and arrows, though the Cherokee also used blowguns with darts for small animals. Their chief game was the plentiful deer. Sometimes hunters set fire to the underbrush in a forest to flush deer out into the open for killing. In addition to meat, the deer provided skins for clothes and blankets, bones and antlers for tools and arrowheads and sinew that could be used for sewing. Other game included bear and wild turkeys. From bear, the

The Indian village of Pomeiooc. *Engraving by Theodor de Bry from a painting by John White, North Carolina Collection.*

Natives derived meat, cured skins and rendered fat and claws for personal decoration. Besides being a source of food, turkeys supplied feathers for individual adornment and ceremonial purposes. Traps could be employed for small game, such as rabbits, squirrels and birds.

Town Creek Indian Mound, a ceremonial site of the Mississippian culture in Montgomery County, North Carolina. *State Archives of North Carolina.*

Men performed the hunting, but both men and women fished. Their methods of fishing included using hooks, nets, spears and traps. Damming streams produced pools in which fish were easily caught. Shellfish could be found in coastal waters. For traveling and fishing, Natives hollowed out canoes from felled trees.

Men and women labored jointly in the planting and harvesting of crops. But in some tribes, women conducted most of the farming. Their major crops were corn (the largest crop), squash, beans, pumpkins and sunflowers, which were supplemented with wild greens, fruits and nuts.

Food preparation included drying, roasting and stewing meat and fish. Corn was a main staple of the Native diet. Some was eaten green, but women customarily soaked, drained and then pounded it into meal for baking bread. Sometimes, they added nuts or beans to the bread.

Clothing for the Indians varied according to the seasons. In the warm months, they wore few clothes and no shoes. Men wore breechcloths or apron-like deerskins, and women wore skin aprons. Children often went naked. During cold weather, the Natives donned moccasins, leggings and warm capes made of skins or feathers.

Indians embraced a religion of spirits and gods who had strong connections to the natural world and influenced events on Earth. They believed in an

Indians fishing. *Engraving by Theodor de Bry from a painting by John White, North Carolina Collection.*

afterlife, where bravery and moral conduct were rewarded and cowards and immoral people were punished. To help them live in accordance with the spirits and nature, Natives engaged in rituals of the purification of their bodies, both inside and outside. Inner purification meant drinking a dark tea, most often brewed from the yaupon shrub. The outer body was purified in sweat lodge sessions followed by plunges in cold streams. Ceremonies could

Indians making a canoe. *Engraving by Theodor de Bry from a painting by John White, North Carolina Collection.*

Indians cooking in a large pot. *Engraving by Theodor de Bry from a painting by John White, North Carolina Collection.*

Indian women holding babies. *Engraving by Theodor de Bry from a painting by John White, North Carolina Collection.*

purify an entire group and honor spirits. According to Theda Perdue and Christopher Arris Oakley, historians of North Carolina's Indians:

> *The major event in the religious life of many native Carolinians was the Green Corn Ceremony. Held in the late summer when the corn could first be eaten, this ceremony commemorated the new crop. It was also an occasion for people to clean the council house and their family homes, thereby symbolically cleaning their environment. They fasted and then bathed, extinguished old fires and rekindled new ones and forgave most wrongs done them in the preceding year. Carolina Indians entered the new year with themselves spiritually cleansed and their social relationships repaired.*

The Natives buried their dead in various mounds and enclosures. A common practice in the Piedmont was to inter the body in a round pit, with the corpse tied in a fetal position. Various items were placed in graves, apparently for use in the afterlife.

Tribal family systems called clans comprised groups of people who considered themselves blood relatives. At the center of the clans were mothers, a position that gave women a voice in tribal affairs. The clan ruled on the behaviors and actions of its members, including deciding who could marry. Each clan had a totem animal, such as the bear or wolf.

For government, each tribe had a chief, who was advised by a council composed of the leader from each village as well as a number of elders. A chief generally did not make a serious decision that affected a tribe without first meeting with the council, which usually agreed on a course of action. Some tribes had one chief for making war and another to govern during peace.

Tribes constantly engaged in war with one another. Reasons for this warfare included attempting to seize the property of a neighboring tribe, settling a dispute over territory or avenging a wrong. War parties ranged in size from a few warriors to more than one hundred. The fighting was brutal, and the dead were scalped and dismembered. The victors dragged some prisoners to their villages, where the inhabitants tortured them to death. When Europeans arrived in North Carolina, intertribal war increased as a means for some tribes to capture rival Natives and sell them to the settlers for use as an enslaved labor supply, along with enslaved Africans. With the exception of deerskins, the sale of enslaved people became the Indians' most lucrative trade with White settlers.

When the Natives first came into contact with the new arrivals from across the Atlantic Ocean, they were primarily accommodating, providing food and furs in trade, instructions for growing crops and skills for surviving in the wilderness. Colonists traded the Natives metal hoes, knives, hatchets and cooking utensils, as well as guns, powder and shot. Unfortunately, they also fortified them with alcohol, usually rum, which had a devastating effect on the Natives, who did not tolerate it well. This frequently made it easy to cheat them in trade.

Very quickly, relations between the two cultures became adversarial, and violent clashes and raids by both occurred often, especially as White settlers increasingly encroached on Native land. The earliest "war" was a two-year struggle between the settlers and the Chowanoc tribe in the region of Albemarle Sound. When the Chowanoc were ultimately defeated in 1677, they were assigned to a small reservation in present-day Gates County. The colonists subsequently fought separate major wars with the Tuscarora and the Cherokee. (Those conflicts will be discussed in later chapters.) White settlers generally triumphed in these armed conflicts, and the Natives' numbers declined and their landholdings diminished.

European diseases took an even greater toll on the Native population, which lacked immunity to these illnesses. Smallpox was especially deadly.

An epidemic in 1695 killed nearly the entire tribe of Pamlico Indians. Another in 1738 claimed the lives of half the Cherokee. Thousands of Natives also died from measles. Perdue and Oakley report that one group of demographers "have theorized that for every one hundred Indians at the time of European contact, only five existed two hundred years later." Tribes vanished as more and more Natives died out or were acculturated into White society. Indeed, from the very beginning of colonization, North Carolina's indigenous population was fighting a losing battle against victimization and tribal disintegration.*

Nevertheless, North Carolina's first inhabitants have left their mark on the landscape. Locales throughout the state are named for Native tribes. Rivers especially, such as the Roanoke, Chowan, Neuse, Pamlico, Watauga, Catawba, Yadkin–Pee Dee and Waccamaw Rivers, are constant reminders of the Natives' centuries-old presence. As an early observer once remarked, "Their name is upon your waters—ye may not wash it out."

---

* Presently, there are nearly one hundred thousand Indians in North Carolina, living in all one hundred counties. They represent about 1.24 percent of the state's population. The state officially recognizes eight tribes: Coharies (Harnett and Sampson Counties); Eastern Band of Cherokee Indians (Graham, Jackson and Swain Counties); Haliwa-Saponies (Halifax and Warren Counties); Lumbees (Hoke, Robeson and Scotland Counties); Meherrins (Hertford County); Occaneechie Band of the Saponi Nation (Alamance and Orange Counties); Sapponies (Person County); and Waccamaw-Siouans (Bladen and Columbus Counties). But the federal government recognizes only the Cherokee as an official tribe. The United States Bureau of Indian Affairs provides services to the Cherokee, who govern themselves on a fifty-five-thousand-acre reservation in western North Carolina. The other tribes do not live on reservations and are directly subject to state law.

2

EUROPEAN EXPLORATION AND THE ROANOKE VOYAGES

When Europeans first discovered the New World of the Americas, Europe was undergoing a major transformation, emerging from the High Middle Ages into a period commonly called the Renaissance (the late fourteenth to mid-sixteenth centuries). The changes in social, cultural, economic and political life marked the beginning of the modern era of Western history.

In the Renaissance, intellectuals and artists known as humanists portrayed a new vision of humankind that drew from the classical civilizations of Greece and Rome for inspiration and emphasized the importance of the individual. That new intellectual awakening was reflected in art, music, literature, philosophy, political thought and Protestantism, as well as new science and technology, including the printing press and advancements in astronomy, navigation, mapmaking and shipbuilding. Much of the intellectual awakening had been spawned from the universities of the High Middle Ages.

In addition, a prominent commercial class of middlemen dealing with imports from the Far East expanded. From such Mediterranean ports as Venice and Constantinople, Europeans had traded with Asia for hundreds of years for silk, spices, perfumes, gold, jewels and other much-desired items. That commerce had been conducted over a slow and arduous land route known as the Silk Road. But by the fifteenth century, Europeans were looking to expand their trade and profits by finding a quicker route by water to China, India and the so-called Spice Islands.

Having the advantage of improved navigation, maps and ship construction, Europeans began explorations to find a route to Asia via the oceans. In the first half of the 1400s, Prince Henry the Navigator of Portugal led the way by sending ships south along the west coast of Africa, looking for a passage to the Indian Ocean. In 1488, Bartholomew Díaz of Portugal sailed around the southern tip of Africa, soon named the Cape of Good Hope, and into the Indian Ocean before turning back.

In 1492, the Italian navigator Christopher Columbus, backed financially by Queen Isabella and King Ferdinand of Spain, launched his plan to reach the Far East by sailing westward. At the time, he did not realize just how far he would have to travel to reach Asia or that a large landmass—the Americas—stood in the way. In October, he and his crew landed on a Caribbean island that he named San Salvador. He believed that he had actually reached an island off the coast of India, so he called the Natives "Indians." Columbus made four other voyages, during which he explored other Caribbean islands and the coasts of Central and South America. When he died in 1502, he still believed he had discovered a westward route to Asia.

Other countries also sent out expeditions in the hopes of finding a water passage to the trade-rich Far East. England dispatched the Italian captain John Cabot in 1497 to follow Columbus's example and sail across the Atlantic. He landed at Newfoundland in present-day Canada. The following year, the Portuguese mariner Vasco da Gama rounded Africa's Cape of Good Hope and reached India, thereby establishing an ocean trade route to Asia. Around the same time, another Italian navigator, Amerigo Vespucci, sailed along the coast of South America and recorded information about that continent, which led mapmakers to name the new land in the Western Hemisphere America in his honor. In 1522, an expedition led by Fernando Magellan, a Portuguese sailor under the flag of Spain, became the first to reach Asia by sailing west. In order to do this, however, his ships had to round the hazardous tip of South America. Thus, European countries had two water routes to the Orient, but they involved long journeys sailing southward and then passing very dangerous capes that could easily result in shipwreck.

For the Old World nations of Europe, the answer to this dilemma seemed to be to cross the Atlantic to find a direct route, eventually called the Northwest Passage, through the New World landmass of the Americas. They competed—often in armed combat on the high seas—to be the first to locate and take advantage of that passage. Although their efforts never succeeded in finding the route, their competition led to their eventual colonization

Giovanni da Verrazano. *State Archives of North Carolina.*

of South, Central and North America. The contest for North America primarily involved France, Spain and England, and it was those European powers that made their presence known in the region that one day would become North Carolina.

The first European country known to have investigated the coast of North Carolina was France. In 1524, King Francis I dispatched the Florentine navigator Giovanni da Verrazano to explore the Atlantic coast of North America and report back his observations. He sailed south past Spain and, near the Madeira Islands, set a course westward across the Atlantic. He sighted land in March 1524 in the vicinity of Cape Fear and then sailed south along the coastline for about 150 miles before turning north again, fearing that if he ventured too far south, he might clash with the Spanish.

As he traversed the North Carolina coastline, Verrazano attempted to land some of his crew at a site below Cape Lookout and near Bogue Banks at what is now Onslow County. Rough surf, however, prevented the sailors from landing their small boat. Nevertheless, one sailor with gifts for the Indians, who had been sighted on the shore, swam and waded toward the beach. From a safe distance in the water, he tossed gifts to the Indians. But he was soon swept off his feet by the strong surf. The Natives pulled the exhausted man up on land. He was at first frightened at being in their grasp and began to cry "piteously." Seeing that, the Natives became upset and started to cry, too. They carried him up the beach to "the foote of a little hill against the sune," where they stripped him and warmed him and dried his clothing by a fire. They were fascinated by his white skin. Meanwhile, the crew remaining in the boat worried that the Natives "would have roasted him at that fire and have eaten him."

But the Indians proved "courteous and gentle," and when the sailor indicated that he wanted to return to the boat, they accompanied him to the water's edge, where they left him and then "went unto a high grounde and stoode there, beholding him until he entered into the boat." That encounter was the first recorded meeting of Europeans and the Natives of North Carolina, whom the White men described as "of colour russet…their hayre blacke, thicke and not very long, which they tye together in a knot behind and weare it like a little taile. They are well featured in their limbes, of meane stature and commonly somewhat bigger than we; broad breasted, strong armed, their legs and other parts of their bodies well fashioned and they are disfigured in nothing."

After that encounter with the Indians, Verrazano's expedition continued sailing along the Outer Banks, ultimately traveling as far north as Nova Scotia. As the Florentine explorer looked over the banks into the Pamlico and Albemarle Sounds, he did not see the mainland beyond the sounds, and he thus concluded that he was viewing the Pacific Ocean and the passage to the Far East. He reported that impression back in Europe, and for more than a century, European maps of the New World depicted the error. Verrazano's life ended tragically when he was killed and eaten by cannibal Natives on an island off South America. His report to the king of France, however, became the "earliest description known to exist of the Atlantic coast north of Cape Fear." It would be published in 1582 in Richard Hakluyt's *Divers Voyages Touching the Discoverie of America and the Islands Adjacent*, and it influenced the future expeditions of European countries seeking to plant colonies in the Western Hemisphere.

After its initial exploration, France did not attempt to colonize North Carolina. It launched two unsuccessful efforts in the 1560s to establish colonies in the area of present-day South Carolina. But its westward expansion was curtailed when it became embroiled in political and religious conflict and war in Europe. France eventually would turn to colonization in Canada, the Mississippi River Valley and what became the territory known as Louisiana, seeking profits in fishing and the fur trade.

The Spanish were more persistent and aggressive in exploring and colonizing the southern part of North America. With authorization from the king of Spain, Lucas Vázquez de Ayllón—a government official, slave trader and explorer—led an expedition from Santo Domingo in the Caribbean to the coast of North Carolina in 1526. His fleet encompassed six ships and a tender. Onboard were five hundred men and women, including three monks and a few enslaved Black people. The vessels landed at the mouth of the Cape Fear River, which the Spaniards named Rio Jordan. There, they established their colony and built one small ship to replace one that was lost during the landing and another craft for exploring up the river. The colony quickly failed because of disease, starvation and mutiny. De Ayllón then moved the settlement to a site on the coast of present-day South Carolina, where it also collapsed from illness and hunger. He died there, and the surviving 150 colonists then returned to Santo Domingo.

Spain, however, remained committed a bit longer to efforts to establish itself in North America. By the late 1530s, it had seized much of the Caribbean, South America, Mexico and the Gulf coast of North America. As early as 1513, Vasco Núñez de Balboa had crossed the Isthmus of Panama and discovered the Pacific Ocean. In that same year, Juan Ponce de León landed in Florida. Six years later, Hernando Cortés invaded Mexico and quickly conquered the Aztec Natives. In 1535, Francisco Pizarro reached Peru, defeated the Inca Natives and acquired the world's richest silver mines. Spain was fast becoming a wealthy empire by grabbing such riches as gold, silver, sugar, lumber and other valuable resources as it decimated Native populations through war and disease.

In 1540, Spain's reach extended into North Carolina. In the previous year, Hernando de Soto departed Cuba with a group of five hundred to six hundred men, horses, mules, dogs and pigs. Landing in southern Florida, the Spaniards traveled north before passing the winter of 1539–40 near what is now the city of Tallahassee. They then marched through Georgia and South Carolina into western North Carolina, where they hoped to find gold. The expedition reached the Blue Ridge Mountains in May, and there, they encountered the Cherokee, who were friendly and provided them with food and support. Finding no gold, de Soto continued his march westward through the mountains, discovering in modern Macon County the Little Tennessee River, which flowed into the Mississippi River. Following the route of North Carolina's western tributaries, his exploration ended on the banks of the Mississippi in 1541.

The Spanish, however, were not done with their incursion into North Carolina. They worried that their French competitors might establish colonies in the Carolinas and become a military threat. So, in April 1566, Captain General Pedro Menendez Aviles established a settlement known as Santa Elena at modern Parris Island, South Carolina. From there, he ordered his subordinate Juan Pardo, with 125 soldiers, to explore the interior of the Carolinas. Pardo and his men marched northwest, following much of de Soto's path and visiting Native villages along the way. In December 1566, they halted for the winter in the foothills of the Blue Ridge Mountains at a Native town known as Joara, near present-day Morganton in Burke County. There, they built a fort and named it Fort San Juan. They also called the site the town of Cuenca. Fort San Juan became the largest of a number of outposts that Pardo established at various Indian villages along his route in North Carolina and eastern Tennessee.

Hernando de Soto. *State Archives of North Carolina.*

Leaving a garrison at Fort San Juan, Pardo and his remaining soldiers traveled back east and established other outposts, where he received word that the French might attack Santa Elena. He and his men then marched back to the island to help defend the town, reaching it in March 1567. The French assault did not occur, however, and in September, Menendez sent Pardo on a second expedition into North Carolina, this time in search of a southwestern route to the silver mines near Zacatecas, Mexico. The Spaniards penetrated a short distance into eastern Tennessee before journeying back to Fort San Juan without venturing farther to look for a passage to Mexico. Then with a garrison of thirty-one men left at the fort, Pardo started back to Santa Elena, arriving in March 1568 and never attempting to return to North Carolina. It is generally believed that Indians destroyed Fort San Juan and the other Spanish outposts and killed any remaining occupants, although some of the soldiers might have died of starvation or sickness. The end of Pardo's expeditions concluded any plans by the Spanish to create a colony in North Carolina, as Spain devoted its efforts toward securing the gold, silver and other riches of South and Central America and the Caribbean.

With France and Spain now directing their efforts elsewhere in the New World, the mission of exploring and colonizing North Carolina was undertaken by England, and it would be that country that would leave a lasting imprint on the land. Compared to its western European neighbors, England was a relative latecomer in planting a foothold in America. But during the reign of the Tudor queen Elizabeth I (1558–1603), it entered the race to secure worldwide power by settling North America and exploiting its natural resources. Although John Cabot had landed there in 1497 and made a claim for England, the country had not followed up with colonization. But Elizabeth realized that she could not allow Spain and France to dominate England in the Western Hemisphere and on the world stage. She wanted her country to obtain its share of the gold, silver, lumber, spices and other resources that were enriching Spain. Already, her ships were on the high seas, many of them captained by "sea dogs" such as Francis Drake, and had been seizing the cargos of Spanish treasure ships loaded with valuable resources from South and Central America and the West Indies. Those raiders were also attacking and destroying some of the Spanish outposts.

Two Englishmen who advised and assisted the queen in her efforts to challenge Spanish power by creating English colonies in North America and tapping their resources were Walter Raleigh and his half-brother Sir Humphrey Gilbert. In 1577, one of them, probably Gilbert, submitted to her a plan titled "A Discourse How Her Majesty May Annoy the Kinge of

Walter Raleigh. *State Archives of North Carolina.*

Spaine by Fitting Out a Fleet of Shippes of War Under Pretence of Letters Patent, to Discover And Inhabit Strange Places." Elizabeth responded by granting Gilbert a charter to discover and colonize "remote heathen and barbarous lands, Countries and territories, not actually possessed of any Christian Prince or people." She authorized Gilbert to govern and profit from any settlement according to his own plan, as long as it adhered to the laws of England. He obtained a number of investors in his venture, and in

June 1583, with a crew and six ships, he sailed for North America. He landed in Newfoundland in August. But disappointed in such a bleak place, he soon abandoned any idea of a colony there. While sailing back home, he died when his ship sank in a storm.

Elizabeth and Raleigh, however, remained committed to English colonization in America. Raleigh found new investors, and in March 1584, the queen issued him a charter similar to the one given to Gilbert. But this time, Raleigh's plan was not to return to Newfoundland but to seek out a site farther south. And that site would prove to be on the coast of what is now North Carolina. Shortly after Elizabeth granted him the charter, Raleigh enlisted two captains, Philip Amadas and Arthur Barlowe, each to command a ship on a new voyage to America to find a satisfactory site for English settlement. Accompanying the two captains was the Portuguese pilot Simon Fernández (also known as Fernandez or Fernando). He might have been the same man, remembered as Domingo Fernández, who had been with a Spanish expedition that, in 1566, had passed through an inlet (possibly Currituck Inlet, later closed) on the northern Outer Banks and gone ashore on the Currituck Peninsula before sailing back through the inlet. If so, he had some knowledge of the North Carolina coastline, as well as the Spanish trade routes.

Amadas's and Barlowe's ships departed the port of Plymouth in April 1584, sailed south to the Canary Islands and then set a course across the Atlantic for the West Indies. Around June 10, they stopped at a Caribbean island, probably Puerto Rico, long enough to take on fresh water and food. Then, eluding Spanish ships and sighting the American coastline, they traveled northward until they reached North Carolina sometime in July. Fernández guided the expedition along the Outer Banks, looking for an inlet into the sounds to make landfall. No one knows for certain where Amadas and Barlowe first landed. A number of historians maintain that it was probably at Ocracoke Inlet, called Wococon by the Natives. Others believe that the site was farther north on the banks, where other inlets might have been open at the time. In any event, the expedition spent a good part of the summer exploring the Outer Banks and Roanoke Island, where they made their headquarters after reaching it by crossing Pamlico Sound.

The crew made peaceful contact with the Roanoac (Roanoke) Natives, led at the time by tribal elder Granganimeo, brother of King Wingina, who was on the mainland recovering from wounds he had incurred in a war with the Neiosioke (Neuse) tribe. The English did not meet Wingina and declined the request of some of his people to help them fight the Neiosioke, who lived in the vicinity of the Neuse River. But they did trade with the Indians, exchanging tin kettles and plates and sundry items for deer and buffalo skins. Barlowe described the Natives as "very handsome and goodly people and in their behaviour as mannerly and civill, as any in Europe."

He also gave glowing descriptions of the coastal islands and their wildlife and resources. They had "many goodly woods, full of Deere, Conies [rabbits], Hares and Fowle…in incredible aboundance." The trees were "the highest and reddest Cedars of the world," and there were so many grapes that "in all the world the aboundance is not to be founde." Barlowe, however, wrote his report with a degree of favorable exaggeration because he knew that Raleigh wanted to use his description as inducement to others to invest in the enterprise of colonization.

In their weeks of exploration, the Englishmen found no gold, silver, precious gems or valuable metals. But they gained knowledge of the topography and flora and fauna of the coastal region, as well as the Indians' methods of farming, boatbuilding, worshiping, housing and conducting tribal relations and warfare. Armed with that information, they set sail for England and arrived there in mid-September. Accompanying them were two Natives: Manteo and Wanchese. Manteo was from the Croatoan tribe that lived on the Outer Banks near Cape Hatteras. Wanchese was a member of the Roanoac tribe.

Raleigh and Elizabeth were pleased with the discoveries of Amadas and Barlowe, and they immediately began making plans to establish a permanent colony in this new land now claimed by England. They named it Virginia in honor of Elizabeth, who was known as the virgin queen because she never married. The English Crown intended for "Virginia" ultimately to encompass as much territory in North America as England could claim and govern. Having not seen American Indians before, the royal court found Manteo and Wanchese fascinating, and the two excited much public interest in the enterprise of colonization. Elizabeth knighted Raleigh; allowed him gunpowder from the government's supply; placed one of her ships, the *Tiger*, at his disposal; and ordered Ralph Lane, a military officer and government official in Ireland, to return to England to assist Raleigh in his efforts to establish a permanent English settlement in America.

In making plans for his colony, Raleigh had the assistance of Thomas Hariot (sometimes spelled Harriot), a scientist, mathematician, astronomer and expert on navigation. Soon after completing his university education, "Master Hariot" joined Raleigh's household and taught him mathematics and navigation. He also instructed Amadas and Barlowe in navigation, wrote a text on the subject and provided Raleigh with advice and guidance on how to establish a colony and make it prosper.

Raleigh assembled seven ships and about six hundred men, half of whom were sailors and the other half soldiers and settlers. The seven vessels were the *Tiger*, *Elizabeth*, *Roebuck*, *Dorothy*, *Lion* and two pinnaces. The *Tiger*, the largest, was captained by Sir Richard Grenville, with Amadas also onboard. The captain and owner of the *Lion* was George Raymond. Captain John Clarke commanded the *Roebuck*. Barlowe may have been captain of the *Dorothy*. Thomas Cavendish owned and commanded the *Elizabeth*. Cavendish served as a member of Parliament, and Raleigh had designated him as high marshal, or the judicial authority, for the expedition. Later, Cavendish would lead a voyage in the circumnavigation of the globe. Fernándes would again serve as a pilot when the ships reached the American coast. The flotilla left Portsmouth on April 9, 1585, bound for the Outer Banks and Roanoke Island. Raleigh did not accompany the expedition because Elizabeth required him to remain in England as one of her courtiers.

Instead, Sir Richard Grenville was in charge of the voyage. The soldier Ralph Lane had the responsibility of final command on land. Two of the most important members of the group were the scientist Thomas Hariot and the artist John White. Both men might have accompanied the earlier 1584 voyage, as some historians believe, but that is not certain. Their names do not appear on the list of the ten signers of Barlowe's 1584 report. Also onboard were the two Natives Manteo and Wanchese. Manteo would live among the White colonists and assist them by serving as a guide and providing information about the coastal area and its Native inhabitants. Wanchese, on the other hand, rejected cooperation with the settlers, returned to his tribe and ultimately fought against the English intruders.

In this 1585 venture, Hariot had the mission of studying the Indians, wildlife, plants, potential crops and natural resources in "Virginia." He ultimately recorded his observations in the book *A Briefe and True Report of the New Found Land of Virginia*. Published in 1588, it was regarded as an important scientific account of the New World and had a significant impact in Europe. Working in collaboration with Hariot, artist John White produced graphic and influential drawings and watercolor paintings of the Native people, landscape, plants and wildlife of America. He also drew and painted maps of the coastal region. His images were the first of America ever seen by many Europeans. The renderings of the Natives and their villages and activities received particular notice and were reproduced in engravings by the Flemish engraver and publisher Theodor de Bry.

The expedition followed the usual route across the Atlantic, led by Grenville's flagship, the *Tiger*. But the fleet soon encountered severe weather in the Bay of Portugal. One pinnace sank, and the other vessels scattered. The *Tiger* continued on toward the West Indies alone, leaving the other ships to trail behind. None had caught up when the *Tiger* landed at the "Bay of Muskito" on the southern coast of Puerto Rico in May. There, Lane supervised the construction of a fort to protect the English from the Spanish while they built another pinnace from local timber to replace the one lost in the storm. The *Elizabeth* soon arrived at Muskito Bay. With the pinnace quickly completed, the three vessels sailed for the North Carolina coast. Grenville did not know whether or not the other ships had survived the storm and would rendezvous with him at sea or off the Outer Banks.

En route, his force captured two Spanish ships, one laded with a large cargo, and stole a supply of salt from the Spanish salt mounds on Puerto Rico's Cape Rojo. The small fleet then stopped at the Port of Isabela on the island of Hispaniola, where Grenville managed to bargain with the Spanish for a sizable supply of livestock, hides, sugar, ginger and other items, paying for it all with the cargo seized from the two Spanish ships. Stopping briefly in the Bahama Islands once to hunt seals and again to look for more salt, the expedition finally reached the Outer Banks at Wococon (Ocracoke) Inlet on June 26.

When the pilot Fernándes attempted to maneuver the *Tiger* through the inlet, it ran aground, and waves washed over and flooded it. Most of its cargo was either lost or ruined. The crew set about salvaging and repairing the ship. In the meantime, Grenville learned that his was not the first vessel from the flotilla to reach the Outer Banks. Some three weeks earlier, the *Lion* had anchored at Croatoan (now Hatteras and Ocracoke Islands). Seeing that Grenville's other ships had not arrived yet, Captain George Raymond deposited thirty men near Cape Hatteras before sailing off north toward Newfoundland, leaving the thirty men to join with the other Englishmen when they arrived. Of the remaining vessels that had been scattered in the storm in Portugal Bay, apparently the *Roebuck*, the *Dorothy* and the other pinnace eventually joined Grenville's fleet.

Grenville dispatched several men to make a preliminary investigation of the mainland in anticipation of a larger exploratory party to follow. Manteo served as a guide. The party came back with a positive report. Then for a more extensive mainland exploration, Grenville selected fifty men, whom he conveyed across Pamlico Sound in four shallow-draft boats and the pinnace constructed at Moskito Bay. Among the principals onboard were Cavendish, Lane, Amadas, Clarke and White. The group had sufficient supplies for eight days.

Grenville and his party sailed along a considerable part of the mainland, going as far north as present-day Lake Mattamuskeet in Hyde County and as far south as the entrance of the Neuse River. They called at three Native villages: Secoton, Pomeiooc and Aquascogoc. Secoton was located somewhere on the south side of the Pamlico River, below what is now the town of Chocowinity in Beaufort County. Pomeiooc was in the vicinity of the current communities of Englehard and New Holland in Hyde County. Aquascogoc probably stood in the vicinity of today's Belhaven and Pantego in Beaufort County. Greetings between the Indians and the explorers were friendly. But when one of the Natives of Aquascogoc evidently stole a silver cup from the Englishmen, Grenville ordered the village and its corn crop burned. Artist John White depicted the villages of Secoton and Pomeiooc in his drawings.

On July 21, the English fleet set sail from Wococon for Roanoke Island. Grenville had notified King Wingina that he was coming, and on July 27, the ships arrived. Two days later, Granganimeo, accompanied by Manteo, visited aboard the flagship. Mostly likely, Grenville and Lane went to the village of King Wingina on the north side of the island and agreed on a site for building a fort and settlement. Relationships with the Roanoke tribe had begun amicably but remained so for only a short period. Around the same time, an expedition commanded by Captain Amadas left to explore Albemarle Sound and the surrounding land. It traveled westward as far as the Chowan and Roanoke Rivers and made contact with several Native villages.

There might have been no conflict with the Indians on Roanoke Island at this point, but the same could not be said about relations among the Englishmen themselves. Considerable dissension had arisen involving some members of the group. Grenville and Lane had been quarreling since Muskito Bay over who had authority over whom. Fernándes resented Grenville for blaming him for the grounding of the *Tiger*. Cavendish, Clarke and treasurer Francis Brooke sided with Lane against Grenville, who was noted for his quick temper. Nevertheless, the two leaders managed to cooperate as Lane built his fort and Grenville made his plans for returning to England for supplies.

No drawings or written descriptions of the fort, named Fort Raleigh, have survived. Archaeological excavations, however, have revealed that the fortification was square and about seventy feet wide. It had protruding

The Indian village of Secoton. *Engraving by Theodor de Bry from a painting by John White, North Carolina Collection.*

points from which it could be defended with cannon or muskets. One or possibly two buildings stood within the breastworks. The colonists did not live in the fort but in houses built nearby. The exact location of the community, known as the "Cittie of Raleigh," has never been found.

Grenville and his fleet sailed for England in late August. He left only 107 men—out of the larger force that he commanded—to defend and maintain the fort and village until he returned in the spring with supplies, equipment and reinforcements. Lane was now governor and military commander of the small garrison on Roanoke Island. He had the assistance of Amadas, whom Raleigh had appointed "admiral" of his enterprise in "Virginia." But Amadas had at his disposal just a few shallow-draft craft and the Muskito Bay pinnace for navigating the sounds.

The first challenge for the remaining settlers was to obtain enough food to last through the winter. Supplies had been lost with the wreck of the *Tiger*. It was too late in the season to plant crops, and even so, the Englishmen showed a greater interest in an unsuccessful search for gold, silver and pearls. They did receive some fish and corn from Wingina's tribe. However, David Stick, an authority on the Roanoke Island colony, wrote that "it is difficult to determine how much of this was arranged through barter and how much resulted from persuasion, fear and force." As time went on, the colonists had to face growing shortages and possible starvation.

Nevertheless, Lane continued the exploration of the coast. He sent an expedition, apparently led by Amadas, northward to the Chesapeake Bay (in the present-day state of Virginia). That group apparently spent some time there, but it is not certain how long they stayed or how they might have interacted with the local Natives.

Deploying their small flotilla, Lane and Amadas, accompanied by Manteo, explored the area around Albemarle Sound, where they visited a number of Native villages along the rivers that flowed into the sound. Sailing up the Chowan River, they stopped at the large Indian town of Choanoke in the extensive territory of the Chowanoc (Chowan) tribe, led by King Menatonon, who was physically disabled. Lane held Menatonon prisoner for a time in order to gain information about his territory and the region and Natives in the Roanoke River area. Traveling back into the sound, the English party then sailed against a powerful current up the Roanoke River. There, the Natives avoided contact with the White men and fled their villages when they approached. As the explorers continued up the river, though, the Moratucks fired arrows at them from the shore but were quickly driven away by gunfire. Out of food, Lane and his crew sailed back into Albemarle Sound and on to Roanoke Island, where they reunited with the settlers on the island around Easter 1586.

The colonists had hoped that, by this time, Grenville would have arrived with supplies. But his ships were nowhere to be seen. As famine and starvation loomed, Lane made greater demands on King Wingina and the Roanoacs for food. But the Native chieftain had limited resources with which to sustain his own people. Lane had always considered Wingina to be dangerous and suspected him and Wanchese of conspiring with other tribes in the Albemarle Sound region to attack the colonists. The relationship between the White settlers and the Natives grew more confrontational. Increasingly, Lane and his men clashed with the Natives, seizing their food and canoes and driving them off with gunfire. Ultimately, Lane attacked Wingina's village of Dasamonquepeuc and killed him. When the soldiers surrounded and fired into his village, Wingina attempted to flee into the woods. According to David Stick, "The soldiers took to the woods in hot pursuit, but it was Lane's personal servant, the Irishman [Edward] Nugent…who overtook the fleeing Wingina and returned presently carrying his head." A pattern had already been set in relations between White settlers and the Indians. European disease had begun devastating Native villages, and Natives were falling victim to colonists' encroachment, greed and firearms. The future did not bode well for North Carolina's first inhabitants.

The fate of the Roanoke Island colonists was also in peril. By the spring of 1586, besieged by hunger and Indian conflict, they were worried about their very survival. But relief unexpectedly appeared when a large English fleet under the command of Sir Francis Drake anchored off the Outer Banks in early June. Drake had been raiding Spanish ships and outposts in the West Indies and at Saint Augustine in Florida. He was on his way back to England when he stopped off the North Carolina coast to investigate the condition of the Roanoke Island garrison.

Seeing the dire straits of Lane and his settlers, Drake agreed to fortify them by giving them the bark *Francis*, several smaller vessels, supplies, weapons and equipment. He also agreed to take the weaker members of the party back to England and leave a number of able-bodied reinforcements. Thus refortified, Lane determined to remain on Roanoke Island and had loaded the *Francis* with supplies when, suddenly, a devastating hurricane struck. The *Francis* sank with the supplies and some of Lane's trusted subordinates, and most of the small craft were lost. Drake's fleet was also damaged, and its supplies were running low. Under these circumstances, Lane and his men decided to abandon the Roanoke Island fort and village and return to England with Drake, who soon set sail. The ships left in such haste that three of the colonists who were not on-site at the time were left behind.

But shortly after Drake's fleet departed, an advance relief ship from England appeared off the North Carolina coast. About two weeks later, three more ships carrying supplies and reinforcements and commanded by Grenville joined the first vessel. He did not know about the Drake departure and searched in vain for the settlers. He found the body of one of the three men whom Lane had left behind, but the fate of the other two is unknown. Grenville and his flotilla then started back to England. Before sailing, however, he left fifteen men on Roanoke Island—"furnished plentifully with all manner of provisions for two years"—to maintain England's small grip in "Virginia."

The first attempt at establishing an English foothold in North America had not met with the success for which Raleigh and Elizabeth had hoped. As David Stick has pointed out, "No gold or valuable commodities had been found. The Roanoke Island base was held by a pitifully small garrison. The once-friendly relations with the native people had deteriorated to an alarming extent." But it was not a complete failure. The island had been occupied for almost a year; Spain and France had not contested the English presence; coastal exploration had extended from the Pamlico River in the south to the Chesapeake Bay in the north; and Hariot's written observations and White's paintings provided vital information for the future. Then, too, only four of the 107 colonists had perished in the settlement effort. It was not long before Raleigh was outfitting another expedition bound for the North Carolina coast.

This time, the mission was different. The first try had been largely an exploratory and military operation, with only men. Raleigh, however, realized that if a colony was going to survive and expand in "Virginia," a traditional social and economic structure would be required. Thus, the new expedition would comprise 110 colonists, including 17 women and 9 children. Lands would be allotted and farmed by families. Raleigh appointed John White to be the governor of the new "Cittie of Raleigh." But it had become obvious that the North Carolina coast was not the best locale for establishing a prosperous English community. Exploration had revealed the difficulty. Landlocked by its geography of the Outer Banks and shallow sounds, the region had no deepwater harbor, important for trade and development. Such a harbor, however, had been discovered to the north in the Chesapeake Bay.

So, Raleigh instructed the new expedition to sail back to Roanoke Island; pick up the fifteen men left by Grenville; install Manteo, who had returned to England with Lane, as a representative for the English claim there; and then sail up to the Chesapeake Bay and plant a new settlement. Three ships departed England on May 8, 1587, with Fernándes presiding as "admirall" of the flotilla. Upon encountering a storm off the coast of Portugal, he left one ship, a flyboat, abandoned in the Bay of Portugal. The other two continued on to the West Indies, where they took on water and livestock. They arrived off the Outer Banks on July 22.

On the following day, White learned that he would not be going to the Chesapeake Bay after all. Fernándes, he said, now refused to take the colonists to that destination. During the voyage across the Atlantic, animosity had developed between the governor and the admiral, and cooperation had become increasingly difficult. It is possible that Fernándes wanted to leave the English ashore on Roanoke Island and turn to raiding Spanish ships. In any event, White was stuck on Roanoke Island, at least for the time being. He and his followers crossed the sound to the island and searched for the men whom Grenville had left the year before. They found no sign of them except for the bones of one who had been killed in a fight with Roanoacs. The fort was no longer standing, but the houses were. White set his men about reconstructing the fort, repairing the houses and building new dwellings. Fernándes had not left the area and instead remained anchored off the Outer Banks until a storm forced him to put to sea on August 21 to avoid wrecking on the banks. After the storm passed, he returned his ships to anchor off the islands.

Meanwhile, the new arrivals to Roanoke Island had fared reasonably well so far, with their dwellings and fort repaired or constructed. Manteo had been baptized and given the title Lord of Roanoke and Dasamonquepeuc. Apparently, that baptism was the first Protestant baptism in the New World. On August 18, a daughter was born to Ananias and Eleanor White Dare, and they named her Virginia. Eleanor was the daughter of John White, and Virginia Dare became the first child born to English parents in America.

Initially, the settlers had little contact with the Natives, which perhaps led them to let their guard down, for before long, some of the warriors of the deceased Wingina brutally murdered one of White's assistants. George Howe was wading in search of crabs when a group of Roanoacs, who had been hiding in nearby reeds, attacked him. They gave "him sixteene wounds with their arrowes: and after they had slaine him with their woodden swordes, beet his head in peeces and fled over the water to the maine." In retaliation, White ordered an assault on Dasamonquepeuc by twenty-four men led by Captain Edward Stafford and guided by Manteo. The attackers caught the Indians by surprise, "shotte one of them through the bodie with a bullet" and were about to pursue the others when they learned that they were attacking not Roanoacs but Croatoans, with whom they were friendly. The Roanoacs, led by Wanchese and anticipating English retaliation, had fled the village after killing Howe. Fortunately, before the assault on the Croatoans could continue, a woman from the tribe, carrying a baby, bravely rushed to the soldiers to halt the pending massacre. She explained to them that the Croatoans had crossed the sound to Dasamonquepeuc to gather corn left by the Roanoacs. She thereby prevented the further bloodshed of her people.

The colonists realized that trouble with Indians would remain a threat to their safety and also that their supplies were fast dwindling. They had arrived too late in the season to plant and harvest crops, even if they could prove successful in growing them. By mid-August they had come to the conclusion that starvation was a possibility if they were not resupplied. On August 22, a number of the leaders convened a meeting with White to discuss the situation. They implored him to return to England with Fernándes and secure supplies and reinforcements. White refused to abandon the settlement and called for the appointment of someone else to conduct the mission. But the colonists insisted that he go. Fernándes was determined to sail back to England soon. At a second conference with White, "not only the Assistants, but divers others, as well women, as men, beganne to renewe their requests for the supplies and dispatch of all such thinges, as were to be done." On August 25, the colonists issued White a written document specifically authorizing him to return to England on their behalf and promising to protect his possessions in his absence, and he agreed to sail with Fernándes's fleet. They also informed him that if they moved their settlement, they would leave some durable indication on the island as to where they had gone. If they were in distress, they would carve the sign of a cross on a tree or post.

When Fernándes announced that he was departing, White boarded the flyboat rather than Fernándes's flagship, the *Lion*, possibly because of the two men's dislike of each other. Despite its diminutive name, the flyboat was a ship of one hundred tons commanded by Captain Edward Spicer. White arrived back in England in November and reported to Raleigh, who began organizing an effort to resupply the Roanoke colony.

He made plans to send a relief ship immediately and follow it with two ships commanded by Sir Richard Grenville. However, with war with Spain

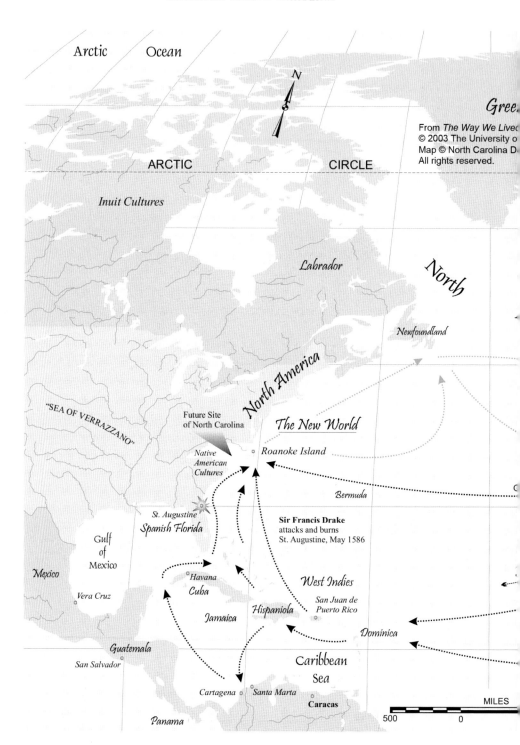

Arctic Ocean

N

Gree.

ARCTIC   CIRCLE

Inuit Cultures

Labrador

North

Newfoundland

"SEA OF VERRAZZANO"

North America

Future Site
of North Carolina

The New World

○ *Roanoke Island*

*Native
American
Cultures*

Bermuda

St. Augustine
Spanish Florida

Sir Francis Drake
attacks and burns
St. Augustine, May 1586

*Gulf
of
Mexico*

Mexico

Havana
Cuba

West Indies

Vera Cruz

Jamaica

Hispaniola

*San Juan de
Puerto Rico*

Guatemala

San Salvador

Dominica

*Caribbean
Sea*

Cartagena ○ *Santa Marta*

Caracas

MILES

500   0

Panama

44

The Roanoke Voyages

Failure of English Exploration and Settlement
1584-1590

Carolina
olina Press
of Cultural Resources

The
Old
World

Iceland

Sweden

Finland

Norway

English
Monarchy   *Scotland*   North
Sea   *Denmark*   Baltic Sea   *Prussia*

Ocean   *Ireland*   *England*   *Netherlands*
London   *Holy Roman Empire*

tic   *Plymouth*   *Paris*   *Vienna*

German
States   *Ottoman Empire*

Bay of
Biscay   *France*   *Papal States*

Azores Is.   CORSICA   *Rome*
Portugal   *Madrid*   SARDINIA
Lisbon   *Spain*   Spanish Monarchy   SICILY

Africa   *Tunis*

Madeira

86

Canary Is.

inds

Cape Verde Is.

Voyages Sponsored by Sir Walter Raleigh:

- **Amadas** — April-July 1584

- **Grenville** — April-June 1585
  "The First Colony"

- **Drake** — Sept. 1585-June 1586
  "First Colony" returns to England

- **Grenville** — May-July 1586
  "The Second Colony" - 15 people

- **White** — April-July 1587
  "The Third Colony" - 117 people

- **White** — April-August 1590
  No sign of *Third Colony* — "Lost"

··········▶ Routes to North America
··········▶ Return Routes to England

MAP BY
MARK ANDERSON MOORE

1000

Map of the
Roanoke
voyages. *North
Carolina Office
of Archives and
History.*

threatening, Queen Elizabeth impounded all ships to defend England. Not until April 1588 did Raleigh manage to send two small ships out of the port of Bideford with supplies and a few new colonists. John White was aboard one of the ships, and the two separated after leaving port. French pirates soon attacked White's ship, killed a number of the crew, injured White and three other colonists and seized the cargo. White's ship then returned to Bideford, and the other English vessel, evidently having experienced some difficulty, soon followed.

Then the Spanish Armada attacked in late July. Raleigh, Drake and Grenville participated in the defense of England. By late August, the armada had been defeated. But it would take Raleigh considerable time to enlist enough investment and support for another rescue operation. Not until March 20, 1590, did White leave Plymouth aboard the *Hopewell*. Also leaving the port were the *Moonlight* and two other ships. Individually, they raided Spanish ships before making a rendezvous in July. At that point, the *Hopewell* and the *Moonlight* separated from the other two ships and set a course for the North Carolina coast.

They arrived off the Outer Banks on August 16. On the following morning, one of the small boats conveying White and others to shore capsized in rough water, and seven men drowned. White and the rest continued across the sound to Roanoke Island, landing there the next morning. As the Englishmen approached the settlement, they observed the letters "CRO" carved on a tree. Upon reaching the site, they saw that it had been enclosed within a palisade made from tall trees. On one of the trees or posts, the bark had been removed, and the word "CROATOAN" carved. But there was no cross or sign of distress. Within the enclosure, the houses had been razed, and strewn about were "many barres of Iron, two pigges of Lead," four firearms, some shot, "and such like heavie things, thrown here and there, almost overgrown with grasse and weedes." White and a few men went to the water's edge, where they found that the boats and pinnace that had been left with the colonists were missing.

At the settlement, sailors discovered a number of chests that had been dug up by the Natives and their contents taken or ransacked. Three of the chests belonged to White and contained some of his possessions, which were now damaged and beyond salvaging. He found "many of my things spoyled and broken and my books torne from the covers, the frames of some of my pictures and mappes rotten and spoyled with rayne and my armour almost eaten through with rust." White surmised that the carvings of "CRO" and "CROATOAN" indicated that the settlers had left Roanoke Island to take refuge on Croatoan, "which is where Manteo was borne and the Savages of the Island our friends."

Before the Englishmen could leave Roanoke Island, a major storm approached, and they fled back to their ships. As the ferocity of the storm grew, the sailors worried that their cables and anchors would give way. So, White and the crew decided not to attempt to remain off the banks and search Croatoan. Instead, they took to sea for safety, with the idea of perhaps returning later to continuing looking for the colonists. However, damage to the ships inflicted by the storm and a prevailing wind led them to sail back to England. Their return to England marked the end of Raleigh's attempts to plant a colony in North America. Apparently, White, who arrived at Plymouth on the *Hopewell* in October 1790, had hopes of returning to search for the Roanoke colonists. But he never managed to acquire the means to do so. "I would to God my wealth were answerable to my will," he lamented as he conceded their plight "to the merciful help of the Almighty." To this day, no one has determined what happened to them.

Their uncertain fate has led to questions, theories and romantic and fantastical legends about the disappearance of the famous Lost Colony. That mystery has intrigued antiquarians, archaeologists, historians, novelists and readers and enthusiasts of North Carolina history for many years. The Lost Colony has been the subject of numerous books and articles, and every year, the North Carolina playwright Paul Green's symphonic drama *The Lost Colony* is performed on Roanoke Island.

Some authorities suspect that the settlers left behind on Roanoke Island migrated to their original destination, the Chesapeake, and were killed by Natives in that area. Others consider it likely that they moved to Croatoan and lived with those Indians. After all, that is what the tree carvings seemed to indicate they planned to do. Perhaps, say some scholars, they migrated inland and connected with Menatonon and the Chowanocs. Or they might have been captured or killed by their enemies the Spanish, who, all along, had kept a watchful eye on the Roanoke Island Englishmen. Given the colonists' bad relations with the Roanoacs, those Natives might have killed them. It is conceivable that they attempted to sail back to England in the small vessels that White had left them and were lost at sea. One unlikely theory, for which there is no real evidence, is that the Lumbee Indians of Robeson County are descended from the Croatoan and the colonists. Over the years, some bizarre proposals have been offered up by opportunists whom David Stick has described as "charlatans" and "quacks." Today, the question of what ultimately happened to North Carolina's first English settlers still inspires interest and research.

But if the fate of the Lost Colony remains a mystery, the importance of the Roanoke voyages in American history does not. After the John White colony did not succeed, Raleigh never made a serious effort to try again or to find the vanished colonists. Thus, one might ask the question: Was Raleigh's attempt to plant a colony in North America a failure? To be sure, neither of his two settlements survived as a permanent English foothold in North America. On the other hand, the Roanoke Island ventures paved the way for future colonization that would endure and help carve out for England a prominent place on the world stage.

Exploration of the North Carolina coast and the Chesapeake region added much to the Old World's knowledge of America, especially as that information was disseminated in the writings of Thomas Hariot and the art and maps of John White. It was spread even wider with greater publicity by writer, geographer and Anglican minister Richard Hakluyt. Known as Richard Hakluyt the Younger to distinguish him from his cousin of the same name, Hakluyt, with some help from his cousin, became the era's chief promoter of English colonization. When Sir Humphrey Gilbert first planned an American settlement, Hakluyt supported his attempt to get a patent from Queen Elizabeth by publishing *Divers Voyages Touching the Discoverie of America and the Islands Adjacent*. When Raleigh took up the patent, Hakluyt wrote and presented to the queen his *Discourse on Western Planting*. He emphasized to her how important colonization would be in enabling Protestant England to gain advantage over Catholic Spain and to procure and sustain economic growth amid international competition. His *Principall Navigations, Voiages and Discoveries of the English Nation* included documents on Raleigh's colonies and more evidence for the importance of colonization in America. He also helped promote Theodor de Bry's first volume of *America*, which included Hariot's writing and engravings of John White's paintings and maps.

With this new knowledge and mission of expansion, the scene was set for England to gain considerable world power through colonization in North America. And it all began on a small island on the coast of North Carolina.

3

JAMESTOWN AND PERMANENT SETTLEMENT

*E*lizabeth I's reign lasted until she died in 1603. Because she never married and had no heirs, the Tudor line of succession concluded with her death. The throne of England then passed to James I, the Stuart king who had ruled Scotland as James VI. Although Raleigh never revived his involvement in "Virginia," he continued to be interested in America for future development and profit. In 1595, he sailed to South America, where he explored the coast of Guiana and the Orinoco River in today's Venezuela. He wrote a book about his experience in Guiana, but he never managed to organize another expedition to South America. The relationship between Raleigh and James I proved to be adversarial, and the king had him tried for treason and executed in 1618. Raleigh never set foot in the land that became North Carolina. Nevertheless, he holds a special place in North Carolina history. Today, the capital of the state bears his name.

Raleigh's Roanoke voyages had revealed the potential of English claims in North America. In 1606, the English Crown chartered a coalition of private investors named the Virginia Company, which formed into two groups to fund settlement and to profit from land and resources in Virginia: the London Company for southern Virginia and the Plymouth Company for northern Virginia. The original investors were merchants of London and Plymouth and members of the gentry in the West Country of England. The Virginia Company's claim in North America extended all the way from present-day North Carolina in the south to present-day Maine in the north.

In December, the London group dispatched three ships carrying 144 people. In April 1607, they reached the Chesapeake. Of the original 144 persons onboard, 105 survived the trip across the Atlantic. In May, they landed on a small island about thirty miles up the James River, which they had named for the king. There was some thought that the river might connect with a long-sought passage through the continent to the Pacific Ocean. Although it was near the riverbank and provided some protection against Indian attack, the island was swampy and rife with malaria and stagnant water. Nevertheless, it was there that the colonists built houses and fortifications and named their new community Jamestown. The settlement was to be governed by a council appointed by the company and a president elected by that council.

Things did not go well for the Jamestown people. Many fell victim to disease, starvation or Indian attack. By early 1608, only thirty-eight of the settlers were still alive. Initial efforts of the London investors to bolster the colony with support and reinforcements proved largely ineffective. It seemed that Jamestown was going to experience the same collapse that befell the Roanoke Island venture. But the London Company came to realize that it must do more to promote the profitability of the Virginia settlement to a wider group of investors by offering land ownership and proclaiming the possibilities of tobacco and other crops and resources. After all, no passage to the Pacific nor gold or mineral wealth had been discovered. The company, therefore, secured a revised charter that transformed it into a public joint-stock company whose members could purchase shares in the enterprise. According to colonial historian Bernard Bailyn:

> In February 1609, its books were opened for public subscriptions and an elaborate publicity campaign was launched to stimulate the sale of those shares, especially in the form of pledges of personal service in the colony by prospective settlers. Such "adventurers of persons" were given one or more shares of stock depending on their "quality" or special skills, each such share to be worth at least one hundred acres of land when, in 1616, the company's assets would be divided among the stockholders.

The London Company also established a new system of government to make the colony operate more effectively. It now appointed a governor who could not be controlled by the council. Originally, having the president subject to the council had led to dissension and ineffective leadership. Only when Captain John Smith, a hardened soldier, seized authority as president and exercised strict control did the colony manage to survive. Smith prevented starvation and kept the Natives at bay. He also conducted exploration in the Chesapeake, including an unsuccessful search for the Lost Colonists, who might have moved to the region. But with the change in the colony's administration, the governor—merely advised by the council—was autonomous and subject only to the English government and the London Company. With new investment by stockholders and more effective leadership for its Virginia colony, the London Company set about saving and expanding its Jamestown enterprise. But like the earlier efforts of Raleigh and his investors to develop a site on the North Carolina coast, not all went as planned.

In June 1609, the company sent to Virginia several ships transporting five hundred men, one hundred women, supplies, equipment and a newly appointed governor and council. But the voyage proved difficult. The passengers suffered rough weather, bad food and disease that broke out en route. The ship carrying the new colonial officers was blown off course and shipwrecked off Bermuda. The four hundred people who landed at Jamestown quickly became victims of more disease and dwindling supplies. According to Bailyn, "They fell into fierce factional struggles, lethargy and despair, and they failed to plant the crops they needed for the coming year. In the midst of rich land, they starved and, unable to withstand disease, died in droves, miserably." By winter's end, only sixty of the settlers were still living. When the shipwrecked colonial officers finally arrived in May 1610, they found them merely existing in deplorable conditions. "Jamestown's palisades were in ruins, the houses burnt for firewood, the last of scraps of food—including cattle and domestic animals—consumed; and the people spoke secretly of cannibalism." With no end of their suffering in sight, the colonists decided to abandon their site and sail home aboard four small ships.

But before they could clear the mouth of the James River, they encountered a relief fleet, which included an additional three hundred men and a new governor, Lord De La Warr. Under his leadership, the colony began a process of economic revival. Back in England, the London Company raised more funds and dispatched six hundred additional men and much livestock and equipment. A more concerted effort was made to turn Jamestown into an agricultural and commercial success. Two new settlements were established at the mouth of the James River and a third up the river at the site of the future city of Richmond. A new set of governing laws titled *Lawes Divine, Morall and Martiall* (1612) leveled strict discipline on the community by dividing the colony into martial law units that enforced mandatory work on public projects and imposed harsh punishment on those who failed to work or render military service.

Under these new conditions, the colony made some marginal progress and began exporting a few commodities such as furs, timber and tobacco. However, profits and a sustainable economy and colony continued to elude the company, which attempted to provide more financial support. But investment and funding dropped as the company grew poorer and the population and productivity of the settlement declined. The London Company made a final effort to salvage the enterprise that had already cost it many thousands of pounds. In 1618, Sir Edward Sandys and new company leaders developed another plan of land distribution to bolster colonization and investment. They derived a system of "head rights," whereby anyone who emigrated or induced someone to emigrate to Virginia would receive acres of land. The new scheme also allowed large shareholders to consolidate their landholdings into "private plantations" or "hundreds," which resulted in an expansion of territory and settlement as these new "subcolonies" spread throughout the James River Valley.

Simultaneously, landowners were given more power in self-government. The old martial law code of 1612 was abandoned and replaced with a new government of civil courts, common law and a representative assembly. This was the first such assembly to convene in the English colonies in North America. It met for the first time in 1619 and comprised the governor, his council and members elected from the private plantations and four planned "boroughs." Bailyn wrote that the assembly stressed "that it would not only express popular grievances, as Parliament had done out of mind, but also protect Englishmen's fundamental rights [in Virginia] as they were known 'at home.'" Although the assembly met only once under the jurisdiction of the London Company, it nevertheless established an important precedent for the future government of Virginia.

The London Company managed to send 4,500 more settlers, including a number of craftsmen, to Virginia to vitalize and expand the commerce of the region through the production of staple agriculture, timber, naval stores, iron, salt and glass. Its efforts met with some success but depleted its finances, which had been raised largely by a lottery in England. In 1621, Parliament terminated the lottery in response to public annoyance. Increasingly, the company had to turn over its properties and corresponding profits in Virginia to individuals who were supporting its colony. The London Company's power and potential prosperity were fast slipping away.

The coup de grâce for the company came in 1622, when Indians attacked the farms along the James River and slaughtered at least 347 of the colonists. In retaliation, the Englishmen launched their own bloody assault on the Natives. Having abandoned their fields in planting season to march against the Natives, a large number of them fell victim to hunger and disease. By 1624, only 1,275 of the 8,500 people who, since 1607, had sought new lives at Jamestown were still remaining in the area. In that year, the London Company gave up its economic experiment in the New World. The government of England revoked its charter and took control of the Virginia colony, including its government and land sales and distribution.

Like its predecessor at Roanoke Island, Jamestown had failed as a venture run by a private company. But unlike Roanoke, it did not vanish. It would survive and endure as a royal colony under the jurisdiction of the Crown of England. Although it had not lasted, the London Company's attempt at colonization had taught England several important lessons for establishing a lasting settlement in North America. Any future colony must be self-sustaining by producing its own food and not relying on supplies from overseas. A successful colony could not survive merely as a project for opportunists, adventurers and gold-seekers but instead had to be anchored on family life and work ethic. Also, individual enterprise, private land ownership, a sufficient labor force and a degree of representative government were necessary for economic and political progress.

The basic structure of colonial government had been created by the London Company and would persist under the royal authorities. The assembly continued as a coming together of the governor, his council and elected representatives, who became known as burgesses. Eventually, the burgesses would meet separately from the governor and council. For most of the rest of the century, the governor and council held the greatest power, including over land distribution and economic regulations. The council also served as a judicial body, and county courts were created in 1643. The English Crown appointed a number of governors who served short terms. But after he arrived at Jamestown in 1642, Sir William Berkeley presided for the longest tenure of thirty-four years. This fundamental format of government became the model for the English colonies established in the coming years, including the colony that would eventually become North Carolina.

By the time of its transition to royal governmental jurisdiction, the economic, social and political leadership of the Virginia colony had become a less "aristocratic" group of men. According to Bailyn, "The leaders of Virginia in the generation after the company was dissolved were tough, unsentimental, quick-tempered, crudely ambitious men concerned with profits and increased landholding." They "established themselves by their sheer capacity to survive on rough, half-cleared tobacco farms and to wring material gains from the raw wilderness. Former servants, yeoman farmers and adventurers of little social status or wealth, they lacked the attributes of social authority, but by brute labor and shrewd manipulation, they managed to prosper." Over time, a number of those planters acquired plantations of large acreage in the James River Valley, and they and their descendants evolved into wealthy, more sophisticated and educated tobacco growers who dominated economic, social and political life in the colony.

The most profitable commodity for Virginia planters was the cash crop of tobacco, the export of which became a viable part of the mercantile economy of England. The first Virginian to plant tobacco was John Rolfe, who had married the Native princess Pocahontas. After the first harvest in 1611, production continued to rise as European demand grew.

Tobacco was a labor-intensive crop, and a severe labor shortage existed in the Jamestown region. To obtain workers, planters turned to indentured servants. Such laborers were people from England who wanted to come to America but did not have the means to pay for their passage. They agreed to work for a certain length of time (generally around four years) for a planter in exchange for the payment of their passage across the ocean. They were bound by law to serve out their indenture. When it ended, they were free to pursue their own lives and interests, with most of them seeking land of their own. About 1,500 indentured servants came to the Jamestown area each year during the 1600s.

In 1619, the first Africans arrived at Jamestown. It is possible that they were not enslaved but were instead indentured servants. In the beginning, most colonists preferred White servants and farmhands, but slavery gradually became a prevalent labor system. In 1640, Virginia had 150 Black inhabitants, some of whom were either free persons or indentured servants. Ten years later, there were around 300 Black inhabitants, and by 1680, approximately 3,000 Black people resided in the colony. As the duration of indenture became shorter and former servants went out on their own, planters turned increasingly to enslaved laborers, who, along with their children, remained the planters' property and permanent labor supply for life.

With land becoming scarcer, as much of it was claimed by wealthy planters, and with the increasing ambition for ownership by a growing population of former indentured servants, the colonists began to look south of Jamestown for new areas in which to grow tobacco. The demand for new land was also driven by the nature of the crop, which depleted nutrients in the soil. A planter, therefore, could grow tobacco on a tract for only three consecutive years before letting that parcel lie fallow to replenish its nutrients. Eventually, people began migrating south into the Albemarle Sound area of what is now the northeastern corner of North Carolina in search of new land and opportunity. As early as 1622, John Pory, the first speaker of the assembly in Virginia and secretary of the colony, explored as far south as the Chowan River and pronounced the soil suitable for agriculture.

In 1625, James I died, and his throne passed to his son Charles I. At that time, the area of present-day North Carolina was still considered the southern part of Virginia, and it remained largely unsettled by White people. But in 1629, King Charles designated the region from Albemarle Sound to northern Florida a separate tract, and he gave it to Robert Heath, his attorney general, as a reward for his loyal service. The English Crown authorized Heath to settle, govern and develop the area for his own benefit. A new colony established there would also further expand England's presence and influence in North America. The new region was called Carolana, which meant "land of Charles." The name was derived from the word *Carolus*, which was Latin for "Charles."

Heath made plans to send French Huguenots and other Protestants to Carolana, but the English privy council thwarted his scheme, as those people were not members of the Anglican Church or Church of England, which was the country's official denomination. He then enlisted forty potential settlers and managed to get them to Virginia, but there his plan collapsed, and they traveled no farther south. Some returned to England. Others remained at Jamestown. Having failed at colonization, Heath transferred his charter and ownership of Carolana to Henry Frederick Howard, Lord Maltravers, in 1638. He, however, had no more success than Heath in creating a colony in Carolana.

In August 1662, a group of religious dissenters from the colony of Massachusetts did attempt to establish themselves in the area of the Cape Fear River, which they called the Charles River. But by the next spring, they had abandoned their settlement, including their livestock, and sailed away. For some time, any permanent colonization of what is now North Carolina would be confined to the state's northeastern corner.

People continued to migrate from the Jamestown area into southern Virginia and the Albemarle Sound region. The new arrivals, by the 1650s, included explorers, hunters, trappers, traders with the Natives and farmers. The first documented permanent settler in what is presently the

A log house typical of those made by early colonists. *State Archives of North Carolina.*

northeastern corner of North Carolina was Nathaniel Batts (circa 1620–1679), an explorer and fur trader who, in 1655, established a trading post beside a creek on the western side of Albemarle Sound in what is modern Bertie County. At that point, the government of Virginia still had jurisdiction over the area, and the governor had authorized Batts to trade with the Natives and conduct a further exploration in the region. A carpenter from Virginia built Batts a house, where he lived while carrying on trade with the Natives. The structure was twenty feet square and had two rooms and a large chimney. The site "Batts House" appears on a 1657 map titled *The South Part of Virginia.* In 1660, Batts purchased from King Kiscutanewh of the Yeopim Natives more land on the west bank of the Pasquotank River, which flows into Albemarle Sound. That deed, recorded in the Lower Court of Norfolk County, Virginia, is the oldest surviving land deed for North Carolina.

By 1662–63, about five hundred settlers from Virginia had established themselves in present-day northeastern North Carolina. New arrivals were pushing farther away from Virginia. In 1662, the Council of Virginia commissioned Captain Samuel Stephens to command the "southern plantation" and authorized him to appoint a sheriff. Among those known to have received land grants in the expanding area from the Virginia government were Batts, George Durant, Robert Lawrence, Thomas Rolfe, Samuel Pickens, Caleb Calloway, George Catchmaid, John Jenkins, John Harvey and Thomas Jarvis. At least four of these men brought enslaved Africans with them into the region and were granted an additional fifty acres of land per enslaved person.

Of these new arrivals, Durant (1632–1693 or 1694) became the most prominent. From the Yeopim Natives, he purchased tracts on the Perquimans River, which empties into Albemarle Sound. There, he established a plantation at a site that came to be known as Durant's Neck. The deeds (1661–62) to his properties were first recorded in Norfolk County, Virginia. As will be discussed, Durant played an early influential role in the government and politics of a colony soon to be known as Carolina.

As for the future of that colony, it is necessary to turn to political events back in England.

4

THE PROPRIETARY PERIOD

*A*s settlers were moving into the Albemarle region, what happened next was influenced by a number of armed and political conflicts known as the English Civil Wars (1642–59). They were largely clashes between the monarchy and Parliament about how Britain should be governed. The wars took place in Scotland and Ireland, as well as in England. Supporters of King Charles I and his right and authority to rule were known as Royalists and Cavaliers. Those who endorsed more power for Parliament and resented Charles as king were often called Roundheads. Among them were Puritans, religious dissenters who wanted to "purify" the Church of England.

Ultimately, the parliamentary forces triumphed, beheaded King Charles I in 1649 and supplanted the monarch with a Council of State in Parliament, dominated by Oliver Cromwell, who had led the rebel army against the British Crown. Parliament continued to operate until Cromwell disbanded it in 1653. He then presided with autocratic authority as lord protector of England, Scotland and Ireland until his death in 1658. His son, Richard, served a short time as lord protector but abdicated in 1659 as the Royalists regained control of Parliament. In 1660, they restored the monarchy, and Charles II, who had been in exile after his father's execution, became king. Although the revolt against the British Crown ended with the restoration of Charles II to the throne, a precedent had been set for allowing Parliament more power in governing Britain.

King Charles II. *State Archives of North Carolina.*

After the Restoration, Charles II wanted to reward some of the Royalists who had helped him regain his kingship. Among those so rewarded were men remembered in North Carolina history as the lords proprietors or the proprietors. In exchange for their loyalty and support, the king gave them a land grant in America that comprised primarily the area called Carolana that his father had given to Sir Robert Heath. To distinguish between the two grants, however, Charles II named his gift Carolina. The document by which he conveyed to the proprietors the region from just below Virginia to northern Florida was the Carolina Charter, issued in March 1663. The charter survives today in the State Archives of North Carolina in Raleigh. In 1665, the British Crown issued the proprietors a second charter that extended the boundaries farther into southern Virginia and northern Florida.

The eight proprietors were Edward Hyde, Earl of Clarendon and lord high chancellor of England; George Monck, Duke of Albemarle, master of the king's horse and captain-general of the military; William Craven, Earl of Craven; John Berkeley, Baron Berkeley of Stratton; Anthony Ashley Cooper, Earl of Shaftesbury and chancellor of the exchequer; Sir George Carteret, vice-chamberlain of the king's household; Sir William Berkeley, the governor of Virginia who had supported the king from that colony; and Sir John Colleton, who had adhered to Charles's cause in the colony of Barbados. Over time, their ownerships in Carolina would pass to their descendants, relatives and other investors.

In addition to the landmass of Carolina, the charter gave the proprietors considerable authority to govern the province, although only a few actually went there. They could pass laws with the participation of the free male population or its representatives. They might also issue executive orders without any public approval. They could grant land; create courts; appoint the governor, judges and other officials; establish a town; raise an army; and conduct war. Although the settlers were governed directly by the proprietary government—whose laws had to coincide with English law—they were still subjects of the British Crown and had the obligations and rights of all Englishmen. The Church of England, or Anglican Church, became the established church in Carolina, but other denominations were allowed. A number of Protestant churches, including the Quakers, would thrive. Through trade and land sales, the lords proprietors hoped to profit as absentee owners from their new enterprise in North America. King Charles claimed one-fourth of all the gold and silver that might be mined in the colony.

The Albemarle Region

Expansion and Settlement by 1733

Great Dismal Swamp

Currituck Precinct

Pasquotank Precinct

Perquimans Precinct

Pasquotank R.

Perquimans R.

Albemarle County

Bertie Precinct

Chowan River

Chowan Precinct

Durant

Roanoke

Edenton
(Roanoke)

Albemarle Sou

Edgecombe Precinct

River

Batts

Alligator R.

Tar R.

Hyde Precinct

Lake Mattamuskeet

Beaufort Precinct

Bath

Pamlico R.

Neuse

River

Pamlico

Bath County

Craven Precinct

New Bern

Trent R.

Neuse

R.

Ocrac

New R.

North R.

Carteret Precinct

Newport R.

Beaufort

Core Banks

Onslow Precinct

Topsail Inlet

Cape Lookout

Atla

Bogue Inlet

MILES

30   0   30

MAPS BY MARK ANDERSON MOORE

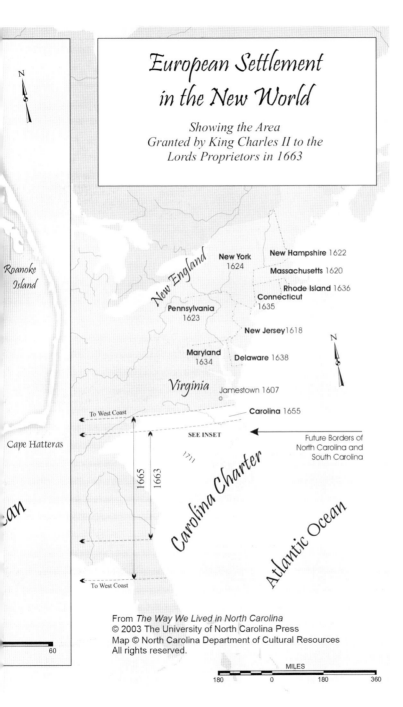

European Settlement in the New World

Showing the Area
Granted by King Charles II to the
Lords Proprietors in 1663

N

Roanoke
Island

New York 1624

New Hampshire 1622

Massachusetts 1620

New England

Rhode Island 1636

Connecticut 1635

Pennsylvania 1623

New Jersey 1618

Maryland 1634

Delaware 1638

Virginia

Jamestown 1607

Carolina 1655

N

Cape Hatteras

To West Coast

SEE INSET

Future Borders of
North Carolina and
South Carolina

1665

1663

1711

Carolina Charter

Atlantic Ocean

To West Coast

60

MILES

180   0   180   360

Map of the
Albemarle
region and
European
settlement.
*North Carolina
Office of Archives
and History.*

Soon after receiving their charter, the proprietors began to exercise their authority over the Albemarle, although at that time, much of the area was technically still part of Virginia. They authorized their fellow proprietor and Virginia governor Sir William Berkeley to select a governor and council for the region. In October 1664, William Drummond, a planter from Virginia, became governor, and in the following spring, an assembly met. Under this arrangement, the government of Carolina "was based on the proprietors' authorizations and instructions." But in January 1665, the proprietors provided for a specific system of government in a document known as the Concessions and Agreement. It divided Carolina into three large counties—Albemarle County in the north, Clarendon County in the Cape Fear region and Craven County where South Carolina is today. These were not like North Carolina's present-day counties; they were actually large districts that included precincts from which the state's modern counties would eventually derive. Each of the three counties was named for a proprietor: George Monck, Duke of Albemarle; Edward Hyde, Earl of Clarendon; and William Craven, Earl of Craven. When, in 1665, the proprietors extended the boundaries of Carolina farther south into Florida and farther north toward Virginia, northward extension helped clarify the boundary between Virginia and Carolina, placing the Albemarle region well within the Carolina tract.

The Concessions and Agreement was the first constitution or plan of government enacted in Carolina. A previous document titled "A Declaration and Proposals to All That Will Plant in Carolina" was written in 1663 but never activated. Under the auspices of that document, the proprietors had hoped to plant a colony of settlers from Barbados along the Cape Fear River. A settlement was established there at a site known as Charles Town, but that attempt collapsed in 1667, and the County of Clarendon remained a wilderness inhabited solely by Indians. With the abandonment of Clarendon County, Albemarle had the only formal government in northern Carolina (that is, when excluding the part that became South Carolina).

Records do not indicate exactly when the Concessions and Agreement went into effect in Albemarle, but it was in operation by October 1667. It provided for a governor, council and assembly, and Samuel Stephens succeeded William Drummond as governor. According to historian Mattie Erma Edwards Parker, "A significant feature of the Concessions and Agreement was the extensive power allowed the popular assembly, which was far greater than that required by the proprietors' charter. Consequently, the assembly was a major governmental agency in the early years of the Albemarle colony," and it "may have been used five years or longer."

The proprietors, however, soon became concerned that they had given too much political authority to the general population represented in the assembly. After all, they were members of the English aristocracy who believed that political and economic power should reside primarily with their class. Therefore, by 1669, they had drafted the Fundamental Constitutions of Carolina to replace the Concessions and Agreement, the purpose of which had been to attract as many settlers as possible. The Fundamental Constitutions, on the other hand, was intended "to avoid erecting a numerous democracy."

With the Fundamental Constitutions, sometimes referred to as the "Grand Model," the proprietors attempted to create a political, social and economic system based on the feudal powers given them by the Carolina Charter. Under such a system, they would have governmental control as well as rights to the land in Carolina. Just below them in status would be members of a nobility with the titles landgrave and cacique, who would hold large tracts of land bestowed on them by the proprietors. Next on the social scale were to be the freemen, who could own land and have a small voice in government. The proprietors and the proposed nobility would own two-thirds of the land, and the rest would be allocated to the freemen, or freeholders. Further down the economic and social hierarchy would rank the leet-men, bound as tenants to the noblemen in a manner similar to the serfs in medieval England. At the bottom of society, enslaved people were to endure being completely subservient to their owners. Noblemen and freeholders would pay taxes to the proprietors. Leet-men, or tenants, would pay rent to the noblemen on whose estates they lived.

According to the Grand Model, the supreme governmental authority was the palatine's court composed of the eight lords proprietors, the eldest of whom was called the palatine. Lower courts dominated by the proprietors and the local nobility were also authorized. A grand council had executive, legislative and judicial powers. The parliament was the assembly for the province, and both the proprietors and the free landholders were represented. Any legislation from the parliament had to be ratified by the palatine and three additional proprietors, and the palatine's court could nullify any activity initiated by the grand council or the parliament.

At the same time that they were issuing the Fundamental Constitutions, the proprietors, urged on by Anthony Ashley Cooper, instigated a plan to settle the County of Craven (modern-day South Carolina), which also would be governed by the new system of government. In 1670, they founded Charles Town (today's Charleston) on the west bank of the Ashley River at a point where the Ashley, Cooper and Wando Rivers converge. Ten years later, Charles Town would move to the present location of Charleston. The coastal region of modern-day South Carolina became a major exporter of rice and indigo from plantations with large enslaved populations. The port at Charles Town was conducive for successful maritime commerce.

Back in Albemarle, the Fundamental Constitutions, which document arrived in the colony in January 1670, along with the appointment of Peter Carteret as governor, did not go into effect until possibly as late as 1672. In the meantime, the Concessions and Agreement continued to operate in the colony.

The Fundamental Constitutions never really worked in Albemarle. Just a few of its provisions were ever enacted. Because the lords proprietors remained a long distance off, the palatine's court proved to be out of touch and ineffective. The intended nobility never developed. Only twenty-six landgraves and thirteen caciques settled in South Carolina, and five landgraves and one cacique settled in North Carolina. A feudal system that might have worked back in England simply was not practical for the sparsely settled, largely wilderness province of Carolina. The assembly of freeholders continued to convene and, over the years, refused to ratify the Fundamental Constitutions. The grand council and the parliament were never established. The proprietors ordered their governors to "come nigh the Constitutions" as much as possible. The Fundamental Constitutions came closer to prevailing in South Carolina than in North Carolina, but it was never completely enforced in either place. With the intention of making the constitutions adaptable, the proprietors revised the document three times, but they ultimately suspended the Grand Model in 1693.

Although never fully enacted, the Fundamental Constitutions did determine the basic structure of the government in Albemarle. The governor, council and assembly continued to function, even though the assembly had fewer powers than it had enjoyed under the Concessions and Agreement. The governors, whom the proprietors appointed and set years of service for, held considerable power. They operated in the proprietors' interest as their direct representatives. They selected the members of the council and all other officials in the colony, and they could remove them without the consent of the council. The governors could also call the elected assembly into session, dissolve it, order new elections and veto any legislation that it passed. The governors had authority over land distribution, legal documents, military operations and relations with the Indians, England and the church.

The council continued to serve as an advisory group to the governor, and it eventually comprised ten members. The governor and the council also functioned as the colony's court until a general court system was created around 1700. Then the general court became the appellate court. The governor and council constituted a court of chancery, and each precinct was administered by justices of the peace. At first, the council and the assembly acted together, with the governor presiding, as a unicameral legislature. But around 1697, that legislature became bicameral, with the council serving as the "upper house" and the assembly as the "lower house." At that point, the assembly began electing its speaker and other officers.

The assembly persisted as the elected branch of the government despite the limitations on its powers. In 1670, Albemarle was divided into the four precincts of Chowan, Pasquotank, Perquimans and Currituck. Each of those first precincts (later counties) could elect five delegates to the assembly. During the proprietary period, no capital or fixed seat of government existed, and the assembly could convene only at a time and place designated by the governor.

As time went on, the proprietors' attempts to turn Albemarle into a successful venture did not live up to their expectations. People were not settling there in the numbers for which they had hoped. The Outer Banks and the shallow sounds prohibited large ships and the deepwater commerce enjoyed by the colony's neighbor Virginia. Communication with other colonies, except Virginia, was difficult. To attract more settlers, the proprietary government lowered land taxes and excused debts and crimes incurred in other colonies. Still, Albemarle remained a sparsely inhabited frontier with bad relations with Virginia, which contested the boundary line set by the charter of 1665. Virginians accused northern Carolina of being an uncivilized "rogue's harbor," a safe haven for thieves, debtors, runaway enslaved people and pirates. Indeed, an element of lawlessness did prevail in northeastern Carolina. The folk in Albemarle accused the Virginians of encouraging the Indians in several of their attacks on the Carolinians.

The proprietors were failing to maintain a strong government in Albemarle to deal with these problems, including Indian uprisings. Throughout the proprietary period, the shortcomings of some of the men who agreed to serve as governor would compound the proprietors' difficulties. A number of their governors were incapable of administering the colonial government effectively, keeping order and protecting the population. Some were self-serving and unscrupulous in dealing with the affairs of the colony. Conflict between many of the settlers and the colonial government had been growing since the proprietary experiment had begun. In 1672, Governor Peter Carteret, at the request of the assembly, sailed to England to discuss with the proprietors how to improve conditions in the colony. Before departing, he appointed John Jenkins, president of the council, to serve as governor in his absence. The proprietors were not sympathetic to Carteret and held him responsible for the problems in Albemarle. He never returned to the province, and Jenkins became the permanent governor.

Amid this contentious atmosphere, many residents of Albemarle openly resisted the policies of the proprietary government. A revolt known as Culpeper's Rebellion (1677–78) occurred as the proprietors attempted to enforce the Plantation Duty Act of 1673. That act was one of England's trade regulations known as the Navigation Acts. Those laws mandated that English colonies use only English vessels to ship exports and that some products had to be shipped directly to England. A number of the early residents of Albemarle, such as John Jenkins and George Durant, had always ignored the Navigation Acts and remained opposed to their enforcement. According to the Plantation Duty Act, Albemarle planters who shipped their tobacco to New England rather than directly to England would have to pay a customs duty of a penny per pound. That cost would inhibit their profitable coast-wide trade with New England merchants, conducted via a few ships from Massachusetts and Rhode Island. The proprietors were committed to enforcing the Plantation Duty Act, especially after King Charles II ordered colonial governors to ensure that all England's trade laws were obeyed.

Governor Jenkins, on the other hand, was determined not to enforce the act. He joined with George Durant in leading opposition to the customs duties on tobacco or other exports. By this time, Durant had become a prominent political leader in Albemarle. For years, he had been a spokesman for the early colonists protesting navigation laws and other policies of the proprietors and the British Crown. Around 1675–76, he traveled to London to explain to the proprietors the dissatisfaction growing among much of the population in Albemarle, warning them that there was the potential for trouble to erupt in the future. After Culpeper's Rebellion, he served as attorney general and speaker of the assembly for Albemarle.

In organizing the movement against the Plantation Duty Act, Jenkins and Durant were joined by John Culpeper, for whom the revolt would be named. He had been surveyor general and a member of the parliament in Craven County before departing that province, apparently in violation of a law that prohibited leaving without receiving permission from the council three weeks in advance. He had settled in Albemarle County by November 1673, when he served as administrator for the estate of the deceased governor Samuel Stephens and became involved in the protest movement against the Plantation Duty Act.

The settlers led by Jenkins, particularly Durant, were opposed by a faction composed mostly of recent arrivals to Albemarle who supported the proprietors and the collection of customs duties. Their chief leaders were Thomas Eastchurch, the speaker of the assembly, and Thomas Miller, a council member and court justice.

As dissension grew between the two parties, Governor Jenkins arrested and jailed Miller. He also attempted to dissolve the assembly, but speaker Eastchurch refused to disband the assembly, which leveled charges against Jenkins, removed him from office and placed him in jail. Miller, in the meantime, had escaped from jail. He and Eastchurch then traveled to England to talk with the proprietors about dealing with the "rebels."

In November 1676, the proprietors accepted Eastchurch's and Miller's account about the troubles in Albemarle. They appointed Eastchurch as the new governor and instructed him to suppress the trade with New England and to establish three ports in the colony where customs duties would be uniformly collected. They made Miller the collector of customs.

On the return voyage, Eastchurch and Miller stopped at the island of Nevis in the West Indies. While there, Eastchurch became enamored of a wealthy widow and began making plans to marry her. As that scheme unfolded, he dispatched Miller to Albemarle to be president of the council and therefore acting governor until he and his new wife could follow behind to Carolina.

Taking up his assignment as customs collector in earnest, Miller collected duties and seized tobacco and other export and import goods on which duties had not been paid. As acting governor, he inflamed the conflict seething in the colony by interfering with elections in the precincts, raising taxes, imposing fines and fees and arresting and jailing opponents. He went so far as to form a personal armed band to protect him from "rebels" and enhance his importance as governor. Many colonists considered him a tyrant. Ultimately, when he arrested a ship captain for importing goods in violation of the Navigation Acts and held him under a large bond, an open revolt, or "rebellion," ensued in December 1677.

Durant and other dissenters made plans to remove Miller from office. The result was that a group of forty armed rebels surrounded Miller's house, captured and jailed him and took possession of his customs records and revenue and any confiscated tobacco. Miller's adversaries then elected a new assembly, which met at Durant's house. The assembly appointed a new council, which tried and imprisoned Miller and some of his appointed officials. The council also proclaimed that if Eastchurch returned and tried to claim the governorship, it would "serve him ye same sauce." It dispatched a group of armed men to the Virginia border to arrest Eastchurch if he attempted to enter Albemarle. He had arrived in Virginia, apparently accompanied by his bride, but died there soon after, possibly from some disease he acquired in the West Indies.

Having seized power, the rebels operated the council and assembly "by their own authority and according to their own modell," and they appointed Culpeper the collector of customs. Miller, however, escaped from jail and fled to England to argue his case with the proprietors. In response, the assembly sent Culpeper to London to present its side of events and justify its actions against Miller. Meanwhile, the British Crown had become concerned about the rebellion in one of its colonies and ordered an investigation and trial of Culpeper for inciting riot. Because they were worried about losing their charter, the proprietors downplayed the seriousness of the revolt, and Anthony Ashley Cooper defended Culpeper in court. He was acquitted. His trial was probably the reason that the conflict in Albemarle became known as Culpeper's Rebellion, although other colonists, Durant especially, had more involvement in the affair.

Conditions in Albemarle remained relatively peaceful for a time, but the proprietors still had to maintain a pro-proprietary government in the colony that could deal with its two opposing factions. They selected as the next governor Seth Sothel, who had become a proprietor after purchasing Edward Hyde's original grant in Carolina. He was familiar with the province and its problems and did not align with either the proprietary or the anti-proprietary group. However, while en route to America, he was captured by Turkish pirates and held captive in Algiers.

In the interim, John Harvey, the president of the council, presided as governor. But he soon died, and the council designated John Jenkins to act as governor again. This gave dominance to Durant and his group. In fact, although Jenkins was governor, Durant actually ran the government. Through his efficient guidance, order was maintained, taxes were collected and laws were passed, including one that pardoned the rebels. Some of Durant's opponents attempted to thwart him but failed. By 1680, it was said, "all things are in quyet" in Albemarle. They would not remain that way, however, as new troubles arose.

In 1681, after Sothel had been freed from captivity, the proprietors recommissioned him as governor of Albemarle. He arrived in the colony in 1683. But he turned out to be the wrong man for the position and one of the most corrupt of the colonial governors. He illegally confiscated estates and other property, stole and embezzled money, bribed and dismissed officials and imprisoned those who were opposed to him. The people of Albemarle had some respite from Sothel's nefarious activities when he visited England for a time in 1685 and 1686. During that period, John Archdale, a proprietor who had settled in Albemarle, acted as governor. But Sothel returned as corrupt as before. Finally fed up with his crimes, the colonists arrested and jailed him. They intended to send him to England to be tried by the proprietors, who had learned that he was not the "sober discreet gentleman" that they originally considered him. However, he chose to be judged by the assembly, which, in 1689, convicted him of numerous charges, banned him from Albemarle for one year and prohibited him from ever holding office in the colony again. Sothel then moved to the South Carolina province, where, after invoking his rights as a proprietor under the Fundamental Constitutions, he took over the governorship. His behavior in that colony was equally corrupt.

For Albemarle, in 1689, the proprietors commissioned Philip Ludwell to succeed Sothel as governor. Ludwell had been a council member, secretary of state and speaker of the House of Burgesses in Virginia. When he arrived in 1690 to take up his duties as governor of Albemarle, he encountered a challenge for the office by John Gibbs, who claimed the right to the position because he was a cacique, a colonial nobleman authorized by the Fundamental Constitutions to be governor. Gibbs had probably moved from Virginia specifically to become governor when Sothel departed. He had, in fact, held the office for a time before Ludwell arrived. Gibbs and a few of his allies attempted to thwart Ludwell by disrupting a precinct court, but the effort failed, and Gibbs took refuge back in Virginia. Quoting Shakespeare's *Hamlet*, he declared that he would "fight him [Ludwell] in this cause, as long as my Eylids shall Wagg."

Finally, to settle their feud about who should be governor, both Ludwell and Gibbs traveled to England in the fall of 1690 to argue their claims before the proprietors. The proprietors designated Ludwell as governor, and Gibbs returned to Virginia. To facilitate their decision in favor of Ludwell, they suspended the Fundamental Constitutions, thereby eliminating the legal argument for Gibbs as governor. That suspension also justified removing Sothel as governor in South Carolina.

When the proprietors selected Ludwell as governor, they extended his jurisdiction southward to cover the "province of Carolina that lyes north and east of Cape Feare." That measure meant that the government of the northern Carolina colony would no longer be confined to the Albemarle but would stretch from Cape Fear to the Virginia border.

In an effort to improve the efficiency of their colonial government, the proprietors then decided to unite northern and southern Carolina under one government. They therefore appointed Ludwell as governor of the entire province, making him the first governor of the entire colony of Carolina. His headquarters were to be located in Charles Town, and he was to appoint a deputy governor for northern Carolina. The original plan also called for one parliament or assembly, which would also be located in South Carolina. However, because the distance between the two regions was so great, an assembly continued to function in northern Carolina. The first deputy governor for that area was Thomas Jarvis, a large landowner and member of the council.

Ludwell's term (1689–91) marked the beginning of a decade and a half of competent and orderly government. It was said of Ludwell that he "understood the character and prejudices of the people thoroughly; and he was possessed of good sense and proper feeling" and managed to "restore a state of comparative peace." That trend was carried on in northern Carolina by experienced deputy governors Thomas Jarvis (1691–94), Thomas Harvey (1694–99) and Henderson Walker (1699–1704), as well as by John Archdale, who served as acting governor of both sections of Carolina in 1694–96 and did much to help direct the administration of the "northern portion of Carolina," where the assembly proclaimed that "his greatest care is to make peace and plenty flow amongst us." All those men were capable and honest leaders who were sympathetic toward the welfare of the population. Walker had served as attorney general and a court justice in the colony, and he was a committed churchman.

By this time, settlers were migrating from Virginia, pushing south of Albemarle and settling in the Pamlico Sound region. In 1675, the population of Albemarle had been around 4,000. By 1700, the population of all of northern Carolina had reached 10,720. The lure of land ownership and the stability of the colony under the past five governors had helped inspire this new migration. To encourage and assist in governing the populace moving south, the proprietors in 1696 authorized Governor Archdale to create a new county called Bath County, which extended from below Albemarle to the Cape Fear and was named for the proprietor John Grenville, Earl of Bath.

It was divided into three precincts—Archdale, Wickham and Pamtecough (Pamlico). As the precincts in this area and throughout the colony continued to grow in number and importance as local governments, they evolved into modern counties, and the large districts known as Albemarle and Bath Counties ceased to exist.

As new arrivals began moving into Bath County, the first incorporated town in North Carolina was established in 1706. John Lawson, explorer and surveyor general for Carolina, laid out the town, which was called Bath. Although it never became large and its importance declined over time, the town of Bath functioned for a number of years as a port of entry and a significant political and trade center. Around the same time that the town was founded, a group of French Huguenots from Virginia settled near the Neuse and Trent Rivers.

In 1710, New Bern, the largest town in Bath County and the second founded in North Carolina, was established at the confluence of the Neuse and Trent Rivers, which flowed jointly into Pamlico Sound. Lawson surveyed that community, too. The story of New Bern began when the proprietors sold to the George Ritter Company of Switzerland thousands of acres in Bath County as part of their efforts to populate the area. The company became aware that a group of impoverished and suffering Swiss emigrants from Bern and a number of war-weary Protestant Germans called Palatines, so named because they resided in the Palatinate region on the Rhine River, wanted to migrate to America. The company hoped for profits in mining and other economic ventures through sponsoring settlement in the colonies. Baron Christoph von Graffenried of Bern, a member and investor in the company who purchased five thousand acres of his own in Bath County, led the expedition of Swiss and Germans who crossed the Atlantic from English ports. The Crown of England, which wanted to place more Protestants in North America, helped fund transportation for the immigrants.

About half of the 650 Palatines who left England in January 1710 perished in the ocean voyage, and the rest were robbed by French privateers just before landing in Virginia. From there, they traveled first overland and then via the sounds to where Lawson and Receiver General Christopher Gale located them between the Neuse and Trent Rivers. In September 1710, Graffenried arrived with around one hundred Swiss immigrants. He found the Palatines in dire straits but quickly took charge, clearing land, building houses and creating a gristmill. He and Lawson laid out a town between the two rivers "in the form of a cross,

Baron Christoph von Graffenried. *State Archives of North Carolina.*

one arm extending from river to river and the other from the point, back indefinitely." Included in the town were a number of craftsmen whom Graffenried considered important for future enterprises. He named the town New Bern for the town of Bern in Switzerland. Within a year and a half, New Bern and its surrounding homesteads were making considerable progress.

But around the same time, an internal problem had erupted in the northern part of Carolina and caused disruption among the populace. The issues that precipitated the trouble were religion and sectional discord between the Albemarle and Bath regions. The difficulty over religion revolved around the establishment of the Church of England (or the Anglican Church) in Carolina, which, according to the Carolina Charter, Concessions and Agreement and Fundamental Constitutions, was to be the official church in the colony, although other denominations would be free to operate. However, it was not until 1701 that the Church of England was officially established in the province. In that year, the assembly passed its first Vestry Act, which allowed for the creation of parishes and vestries and levied a tax to support the clergy. Most Anglicans supported the act, and they established parishes in Chowan, Perquimans and Pasquotank Precincts in the Albemarle. But Quakers, who existed in large numbers in the colony and held considerable power in the assembly, protested against a law that provided for an officially dominant church and new taxes to support that church. Presbyterians and even a few Anglicans joined them in opposition. They were mollified for a time when the proprietors rejected the Vestry Act on the grounds that it gave too much power to the vestry and failed to allow sufficient pay to the clergy.

In 1703, however, Governor Henderson Walker, a devout Anglican, managed, despite the opposition of a large contingent of Quaker legislators, to have the assembly pass another Vestry Act. That law required all members of the assembly to take an oath that they were communicants of the Church of England. The Quakers refused to take the oath, claiming it denied them their right of affirmation. When Robert Daniel succeeded Walker as governor in 1704, he continued to support the oath requirement. But the issue raised enough public opposition that the Presbyterians in the assembly joined with the Quakers and had Daniel removed from office in 1705.

The next governor, Thomas Cary, was thought at first to be sympathetic to religious dissenters. However, he opposed the Quakers and enforced the oath law, thus denying Quakers seats in the assembly. He went even further by imposing a five pound fine on Quakers who held any office in the province and did not take the oath. The Quakers responded by sending a representative, John Porter, to England to argue their rights before the proprietors. Influenced by Archdale, himself a Quaker, the proprietors ordered all laws regarding oaths suspended and Cary removed from office. When Porter returned with the order, Cary was away in South Carolina, and William Glover, the president of the council, was serving in his place as deputy governor in the north. Glover refused to admit new members of the council who did not take the oath. Ironically, the Quakers then formed an alliance with Cary, who, by then, had changed sides and become supportive of their cause, and demanded that Glover be removed from office. But he refused to leave the position, and two factions or parties formed, even threatening armed conflict.

They decided, however, to submit their arguments to the voters. When an election for the assembly was held in October 1708, the Cary/Quaker party, led by the speaker of the assembly, Edward Moseley, prevailed. A still-defiant Glover left for Virginia. Cary reassumed the office of deputy governor in northern Carolina and remained in power until 1711. His faction controlled the government, and many Quakers served in the assembly and held other government offices.

It was during this upheaval that, as the influx of settlers increased in the Albemarle and Pamlico Sounds regions, the proprietors, in an attempt to deal more effectively with governance and internal problems in Carolina, decided to divide the colony into two separate colonies—South Carolina and North Carolina—each having its own government and chief executive. The first governor of the colony of North Carolina was Edward Hyde (not the same person as the proprietor of the same name). He had arrived in Virginia in August 1710, after a voyage from England, and he received his official commission as governor of North Carolina in 1712.

But in the meantime, Cary and the Quakers lost their hold on the assembly. In March 1711, it reinstituted "all such laws made for the establishment of the [Anglican] Church" and levied a fine of one hundred pounds on officials who did not adhere to the laws "now in force." It abolished all the laws passed by Cary's previous government. In response, Cary organized in Bath County, where he lived, a force of "great guns and other warlike stores," as well as a "Brigantine of six guns" and other vessels "equipped in warlike manner." Graffenried, a member of the council, described Cary as "an open and declared rebel" who had "brought together a gang of tramps and rioters by means of promise and by means of good liquor, rum and brandy, to which he treated the rabble, he secured many adherents and they finally came to open rebellion against Mr. Hyde."

In May, Governor Hyde led a group of 150 men to Bath County to capture Cary, but Cary's band drove them off with artillery fire. Cary and his followers then sailed to the Albemarle, where they intended to unseat Hyde by force. On June 30, from aboard ship, they fired cannon at a plantation house where Hyde and some of his supporters, including Graffenried, were meeting. That attack was repulsed, and further attempts were thwarted when Governor Alexander Spotswood of Virginia sent troops to help defend Hyde. Cary and a number of his lieutenants escaped into Virginia but were arrested there in July and sent to England to stand trial for insurrection. Because no witnesses appeared to testify against them, they were released. That ended the so-called Cary Rebellion. Cary returned to his home in Bath County and lived there until his death around 1720. The outcome for many Quakers was a denial of political office, because they refused to take the oath to the Church of England.

Although the Cary Rebellion began as a religious dispute, it also had political implications involving sectional conflict between the Albemarle and Bath areas. Albemarle had been the first region settled, and it had the most precincts and the most political power. Its chief commerce was in tobacco, and it had close ties with the Chesapeake. It also was influenced by the government in Virginia, which had been a royal colony governed directly by the British Crown since 1624. Albemarle's inhabitants tended to support Hyde and the Church of England. Cary's rebels came largely from Bath, which had fewer precincts and less of a political voice, and they supported the Quakers. Bath's largest trade was in animal skins with the Natives. As will be seen, this type of sectional discord would continue to emerge in North Carolina's politics throughout the colonial era.

Almost simultaneously with the Cary Rebellion, war broke out between White colonists and the Tuscarora Indians in the coastal plain. In fact, the Tuscarora seized on the upheaval among the colonists caused by the rebellion to stage an uprising against the ever-growing population of Europeans. The Tuscarora, who were Iroquoian, were the largest, best organized and most powerful tribe in eastern North Carolina. Sometime prior to English settlement, they had migrated from the region of modern-day New York and occupied territory along the Roanoke, Pamlico, Neuse and Trent Rivers, where they established their villages, or "towns." Their hunting grounds reached as far south as the Cape Fear. Their population in North Carolina totaled about 4,000, including 1,200 "fighting men." They consisted of two groups or "towns." The Upper Towns, led by King Tom Blount, were located on the upper Neuse, Pamlico and Roanoke Rivers. The Lower Towns, led by King Hancock, occupied land along the lower Neuse River. The Upper Towns continuously had good relations with the colonists. But the worsening relationship between the Lower Towns and the growing population of White settlers resulted in warfare that lasted from 1711 to 1713.

The war grew out of clashes over trade, land encroachment and mistreatment and enslavement of the Indians. For some time, the Tuscarora had been carrying on a significant trade in animal skins (particularly deerskins) with White settlers, who frequently cheated them, a fact observed by Graffenried and others who noted the colonists' "irregular" and "sharp" dealings. Increasingly, White settlers intruded on Tuscarora hunting grounds and seized their land with little or no payment. The enslavement of the Natives was so extensive that the Pennsylvania legislature outlawed "the further importation of Indian slaves from Carolina." John Lawson admitted the following about the Tuscarora: "They are really better to us than we have been to them." Receiving no redress of their increasing discontent from authorities in North Carolina, the Tuscarora petitioned the governor of Pennsylvania for some relief from their abuse. But their attempts at a peaceful resolution of their troubles were not unlimited, and they had the capacity and temperament for waging major warfare against their enemies. According to Lawson, "The Indians are very vengeful and never forget an injury done, until they have received Satisfaction." Ultimately, declared William Byrd of Virginia, "the Indians grew weary and tired of the Tyranny and Injustice with which the whites treated them and resolved to endure the bondage no longer." So, a tragic and bloody war erupted on the Carolina frontier.

A prelude to open battle occurred in September 1711, as Graffenried and Lawson explored along the Neuse River north of New Bern. Suddenly, a band of Tuscarora took them captive. They soon released Graffenried but killed Lawson by burning him to death. Before Graffenried could return to New Bern and sound the alarm about a pending Indian assault, the Tuscarora attacked the White settlements along the Neuse and Pamlico Rivers. At dawn on September 22, about 500 well-armed warriors rushed from the woods and began murdering, scalping and burning White families in their homes. At least 130 colonists were killed. The Tuscarora mutilated settlers' bodies, plundered and burned houses, killed or drove off livestock, destroyed crops and took some prisoners. Those settlers who survived the attacks fled to New Bern, Bath and surrounding fortified plantations for protection. Not feeling secure, however, the inhabitants of New Bern later sought safety on the nearby fortified plantation of William Brice. The Albemarle region escaped the devastation because King Tom Blount and the Upper Towns did not join the Lower Towns in the fight but remained neutral. Nevertheless, the entire colony was vulnerable.

Governor Hyde found himself having to act quickly and effectively to save the colony from annihilation. But he had few resources with which to respond to the Tuscarora rampage. Amid the hostilities, little trade could

The Tuscarora's capture of John Lawson. *State Archives of North Carolina.*

be carried out, and North Carolina had serious debt, so raising a fighting force was difficult. Many men refused to serve in the militia. Hyde called the assembly into session. It raised some funds by passing a law to print £4,000 in paper money—the first in North Carolina. Other legislation drafted all men between the ages of sixteen and sixty into the militia. Quakers, who were pacifists, and others who could not fight were required to pay £5 each to support the war effort. Hyde managed to organize the militia and established a few forts. But his efforts were not sufficient to defeat the Tuscarora, and he called upon Virginia and South Carolina for help. Governor Alexander Spotswood of Virginia dispatched his militia to the border, but he declined to order them farther unless North Carolina would take responsibility for supplying those troops and agree to relinquish to Virginia a border area in dispute between the two colonies. Governor Hyde refused those terms.

South Carolina, on the other hand, was more willing to help its neighbor. Its assembly allotted £4,000 in aid and sent troops without first demanding "a mortgage or other security." Colonel John Barnwell (known as Tuscarora Jack) assembled thirty White settlers and about five

John Lawson, Christoph von Graffenried and a man of African descent were held captive by the Tuscarora. The Indians burned Lawson to death. *State Archives of North Carolina.*

hundred "friendly Indians," mostly Yemasee, marched three hundred miles into North Carolina and defeated a number of the Tuscarora in two battles near New Bern in January 1712. About two hundred North Carolina militiamen then joined him, and the combined force attacked King Hancock's main stronghold and fort at the Native town of Catechna, near present-day Snow Hill in Greene County.

Surrounded by Barnwell's men and bombarded by their cannon for ten days, Hancock proposed a truce. The terms of the truce that he and Barnwell agreed on were that Hancock would release the White prisoners he was holding, cease attacking settlements and "quit all pretensions to planting, fishing, hunting or ranging all lands lying between Neuse River and Cape Feare."

North Carolina officials had wanted Barnwell to crush the Tuscarora and were so displeased with him for agreeing to such terms that they refused to honor the promise of a land grant for his service. Having been wounded and suffering considerable loss of his own money in the campaign, Barnwell was incensed at "such unkind usage." To secure some profit for their efforts, Barnwell and his men, including the Yemasee, enslaved some Tuscarora and took them back to South Carolina to sell.

The truce did not last, and in the summer of 1712, the Tuscarora renewed their attacks on White settlements. At the same time, a yellow fever epidemic broke out and claimed the lives of many of the colonists, including Governor Hyde. Thomas Pollock, the president of the council, succeeded him as acting governor and again quickly requested help from South Carolina to combat the Tuscarora. Colonel James Moore and a contingent of thirty-three White settlers and around one thousand friendly Indians marched from South Carolina to the Neuse River area. On March 25, 1713, Moore's men and the North Carolina militia won a "glorious victory" over Hancock's warriors at the Tuscarora's Fort Neoheroka, located on Contentnea Creek and near Catechna.

According to Pollock, Moore's force suffered 52 men killed and 82 wounded. The Tuscarora casualties included 200 "Killed and Burnt" inside the fort and 106 killed or captured outside the fort, with a total of 392 prisoners and 192 scalps taken in the battle. King Hancock survived the fight, but King Tom Blount took him prisoner and turned him over to the colonists, who killed him immediately. Because Blount and his followers remained peaceful during the war, the North Carolina government rewarded them with a sizable reservation later known as Indian Woods in present-day Bertie County. The survivors among those Tuscarora who had made war left North Carolina and settled among the Iroquoian tribes in New York and Canada.

At the conclusion of the Tuscarora War, North Carolina found itself in critical condition. Many White settlers and Tuscarora had been killed. Immigration and trade had virtually vanished. Homes and outbuildings had been burned, crops and land laid waste and livestock had been killed or driven off. The war had brought on considerable debt, which the government could not pay with the colony's revenue from taxes. The scarcity of specie left many colonists in financial straits, as the proprietors required hard currencies for taxes and quitrents (annual payments of a tax or tithe by landowners, based on acreage, to the proprietors). The demand of specie for taxes would be an ongoing problem for the colony, leading to opposition from the colonists.

But signs of improvement appeared. Commerce and settlement revived. Thomas Pollock's leadership brought a degree of unity to the colony, which had a more effective government now that it was no longer tied to South Carolina. As Charles Eden succeeded Pollock as governor in 1714, North Carolina entered a period of rebuilding and new advancement. In 1715, the assembly revised some old laws and passed about sixty new ones, which better defined the specific duties and powers of government

Cultures Clash

*European Settlement Pushes
the Tuscarora Nation to the
Breaking Point*

THE TUSCARORA WAR — Main Events

1710
Colonial town of New Bern displaces Tuscarora village of Chattoka

1711
Mid-September — John Lawson is executed near the village of Catechna
September 22 — Tuscarora Indians, in alliance with members of displaced
coastal tribes, attack colonists along the Neuse, Pamlico, and Trent Rivers
October 27 —South Carolina resolves to raise troops to fight the Tuscaroras

1712
January 28 — The Barnwell Expedition crosses the Cape Fear River
January 30 — Barnwell's force destroys the Tuscarora village of Narhantes
February 6 — Barnwell reaches the Pamlico River
February 10-26 — Barnwell's force remains idle at Bath
February 27 — Barnwell moves on Fort Hancock at Catechna
April 7 — Siege of Fort Hancock
April 17 — Fort Hancock falls to Barnwell's force
August 8 — South Carolina sends the Moore Expedition to North Carolina
Early December — Moore's force reaches Fort Barnwell, then moves
via New Bern and Bath to Albemarle County

1713
January 17 — Moore's force advances from Albemarle County
March 1 — Siege of Fort Neoheroka
March 20-23 — Final attack and capture of Fort Neoheroka

Map of the Tuscarora War. *North Carolina Office of Archives and History*.

PRINCIPAL I
Ca. 1600-1700,
Tuscarora. (Eas
displaced by wh

☼ Forts

▲ **Indian Wo**
Reservation
for Tuscaro
Carolina fol
1711-1713.

○ *Principal E*
1690-1733

BARNWELL
Col. John Ba
495 Indians:
33 white colo

MOORE EX
Col. James M
900 Indians
33 white mili

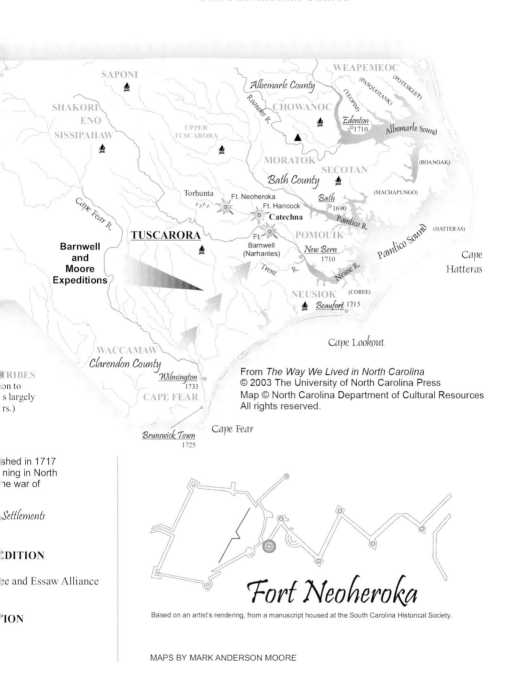

SAPONI

SHAKORI
ENO
SISSIPAHAW

UPPER
TUSCARORA

WEAPEMEOC

Albemarle County

(PASQUOTANK)

(POTESKEET)

(YEOPIM)

CHOWANOC

Edenton
1710

Albemarle Sound

Roanoke R.

MORATOK

(ROANOAK)

SECOTAN

Bath County

(MACHAPUNGO)

Torhunta

Ft. Neoheroka

Ft. Hancock

Catechna

Bath
1690

Pamlico R.

Cape Fear R.

TUSCARORA

Barnwell
and
Moore
Expeditions

Ft.
Barnwell
(Narhantes)

POMOUIK

New Bern
1710

Pamlico Sound

(HATTERAS)

Cape
Hatteras

Trent R.

Neuse R.

NEUSIOK

(COREE)

Beaufort 1715

Cape Lookout

WACCAMAW

Clarendon County

Wilmington
1733

CAPE FEAR

From *The Way We Lived in North Carolina*
© 2003 The University of North Carolina Press
Map © North Carolina Department of Cultural Resources
All rights reserved.

Brunswick Town
1725

Cape Fear

TRIBES
on to
s largely
rs.)

shed in 1717
ning in North
he war of

Settlements

:DITION

e and Essaw Alliance

'ION

Fort Neoheroka

Based on an artist's rendering, from a manuscript housed at the South Carolina Historical Society.

MAPS BY MARK ANDERSON MOORE

Blackbeard the pirate. *State Archives of North Carolina.*

officials. New Vestry Acts protected the rights of the Quakers and other religious dissenters and allowed them to hold political office. Some legislation provided for the construction of roads, bridges and ferries and the designation of channels in the sounds.

New port towns were established. Edenton on Albemarle Sound was laid out in 1712, and its first lot was sold two years later. Originally known as the Town on Queen Anne's Creek, it was incorporated and named Edenton in 1723 in honor of Governor Eden. Beaufort—in present-day Carteret County and named for the Duke of Beaufort, a proprietor—was surveyed in 1713 and soon inhabited. It stood on the site of a former Native village, Warlock, a name thought to mean "fish town" or "fish village." For a time, settlers referred to it as Fish Town. The colonial government incorporated Beaufort in 1723.

Despite this degree of progress, North Carolina still faced an old challenge that had long hampered its development: piracy. Some historians have referred to the years between 1689 and 1718 as the Golden Age of Piracy. From the colony's earliest days, its residents had often ignored and defied England's Navigation Acts, or trade laws, and a good deal of smuggling occurred. Furthermore, there had not been always a clear distinction between privateering, which was legal, and piracy, which was not. As long as colonial sailors raided the ships of England's enemies, the Spanish and French, the act was considered privateering and a loyal service to the British Crown. Seizing the cargos of English vessels was another matter, and pirates did not make a distinction. The Outer Banks, sounds and estuaries of coastal North Carolina provided excellent sites for pirates to hide and suddenly emerge to capture ships laden with goods.

The most infamous pirate who operated out of North Carolina's waters was Edward Thatch (or Teach), known as Blackbeard due to his long, sinister-looking black beard and hair. To enhance his frightful appearance and terrify ships' crews, he placed smoking rope in his hair and armed himself with "three Brace of Pistols, hanging in Holsters like Bandoliers." One observer said that "his Eyes, naturally looking fierce and wild, made him all together such a figure, that Imagination cannot form an idea of a Fury from Hell to look more frightful." Little is known about Blackbeard's early life. Historian Lindley S. Butler, an authority on piracy in North Carolina, wrote, "Although extensive searches by scholars in Bristol, Jamaica and London have unearthed nothing about him or his origins, as a merchant seaman, he surely passed through the major ports of England and the colonies, and it is expected that he spent some time in Jamaica, since the island had a long history as a pirate and privateer stronghold." Blackbeard's first certain appearance in written history was in Jamaica as a seaman aboard an English privateer commanded by Captain Benjamin Hornigold, from whom a number of pirates first learned their trade.

Blackbeard made his headquarters in the town of Bath, where he found he was welcomed or at least tolerated by the inhabitants, who bought and sold some of his loot. Governor Eden had his residence in the town. Tobias Knight, a secretary, customs officer and chief justice of the colony, stored some of Blackbeard's stolen goods in his barn and was accused of being involved with the pirate, but Knight died before a complete investigation could be made.

Another notorious pirate who plundered off the coasts of the Carolinas and Virginia was Stede Bonnet, "the most unlikely pirate who ever sailed the high seas." Before taking up a career of maritime crime, Bonnet had been a wealthy planter and a "Gentleman of Grand Reputation" in Barbados. It is not clear exactly why he suddenly left Barbados and his wife and family to become a pirate. But one common theory held that "this humour of going a Pyrating proceeded from a Disorder in his Mind, which had been too visible in him some Time before this wicked undertaking and which is said to have been occasioned by some Discomforts he found in the Married State." Bonnet differed from other pirate captains in that he paid his crews and had little knowledge of seamanship, which forced him to rely on his subordinate officers. Nevertheless, he managed to outfit and arm vessels and reap a rich harvest of ocean cargos before South Carolina finally put an end to his marauding. In September 1718, Governor Robert Johnson assigned Colonel William Rhett the task of locating Bonnet and bringing him to justice. Rhett's flotilla encountered Bonnet at the mouth of the Cape Fear River and, after winning a five-hour battle, took him captive and transported him to Charles Town to stand trial. Bonnet was convicted and hanged. Some forty-nine other pirates were also hanged in Charles Town in November and December 1718.

At around that same time, Blackbeard and his crew suffered a similar outcome to their careers. The task of bringing down Blackbeard ultimately fell to the Virginians, who had become fed up with his raiding of their maritime shipping from his safe harbor in North Carolina. In the fall of 1718, Governor Spotswood dispatched two vessels commanded by Lieutenant Robert Maynard of the Royal Navy to seek out and attack Blackbeard. On November 22, Maynard encountered Blackbeard's ship the *Adventurer* at Ocracoke Inlet. In the ensuing battle, Maynard and the

Blackbeard's head was displayed as a warning to other pirates. *State Archives of North Carolina.*

pirate fought hand to hand, and Maynard killed Blackbeard. He cut off his head, hung it from his ship's bow and sailed into Bath to demonstrate what fate awaited pirates. In the fighting, Maynard's men killed half of Blackbeard's crew. Nine of the pirates were tried, convicted and hanged in Virginia. With these executions, the Golden Age of Piracy came to an end in North Carolina. (In November 1996, divers discovered in Beaufort Inlet a sunken vessel believed to be *Queen Anne's Revenge*, one of Blackbeard's ships. Since that time, the wreck has undergone underwater archaeological exploration and excavations of its artifacts.)

With an end to piracy and the Tuscarora wars, migration into North Carolina resumed significantly as new arrivals spread throughout the colony, gradually settling farther away from the established towns and communities. During the administration of new arrival Governor George Burrington (1724–25), immigration reached its highest point thus far. Perhaps as many as one thousand families moved into the colony in those years. Burrington urged the building and improvement of roads and harbors and initially had the support of other officials, such as Chief Justice Christopher Gale and former governor Thomas Pollock. But Burrington, who had a violent temper, subsequently made threats and attacks against Gale, which led the chief justice and several members of the council to bring charges against the governor to the proprietors. The proprietors removed Burrington from office and replaced him with Sir Richard Everard, a proprietor, who served as governor until 1731. As the population of the province increased during Burrington's and Everard's administrations, four new counties were created: Bertie (1722), Carteret (1722), Tyrrell (1729) and New Hanover (1729).

It was in New Hanover County that the Cape Fear River Valley would finally be settled. After the failure of the 1667 colony in the old County of Clarendon, the proprietors closed the land office there and, for years, made no effort to develop it. After the Tuscarora War, however, that situation changed. During the conflict, James Moore, his brother Maurice and other South Carolinians who had marched through the Cape Fear developed an interest in acquiring land and settling the region. Some investors in North Carolina also began to see potential profits in what had been wilderness. Around 1723, a number of settlers and investors began to make claims, clear land and build houses on this land. Although the land office had been ordered closed by the proprietors and the British Crown, Governor Burrington nevertheless complied with the instructions of the assembly and reopened the office, which allotted tracts to newcomers. On the Cape Fear River in 1725, Maurice Moore laid out the community of Brunswick, from which the towns of Brunswick and Wilmington and the Port of Brunswick would later derive (see chapter 5).

During this period of expansion, North Carolina and Virginia settled the long-standing argument about the boundary line between the two colonies. Virginia had always held that the proprietors' extension of the Carolina boundaries in 1665 had claimed some territory that actually belonged to Virginia. Since then, arguments over land, taxes and governmental authority in the disputed area had continued. In 1681 and 1699, the British Crown ordered that the boundary be determined, but Virginia refused to comply. When Queen Anne ordered the survey again in 1709, Virginia again declined to cooperate. Finally in 1727, both colonies agreed to conduct a survey. Governor Richard Everard appointed four North Carolina commissioners to partner with Virginia's commissioners in carrying out the work. The prominent planter William Byrd II led the Virginia delegation in the joint effort to "run the line." He would record his experience in his famous *History of the Dividing Line betwixt Virginia and North Carolina*. The survey began at Currituck Inlet on March 5, 1728, and ran 161 miles westward. At that point, claimed the Virginians, the North Carolina commissioners had grown tired and, having "drunk up" all the available spirits, went home. The Virginians, wanting "to complete the Line," ran it another 72 miles, as far as present-day Stokes County in North Carolina. In the end, the results favored North Carolina. Its commissioners announced that "there was taken by the Line into Carolina a very great Quantity of Lands and Number of Families that before had been under Virginia." The governor of Virginia observed, however, that to his colony's "great surprise, it is now found that instead of gaining a large Tract of Land in North Carolina, the line comes rather nearer to Virginia than that which Carolina has always allowed to be our bounds."

By the time the boundary line was determined, the lords proprietors had decided to sell North Carolina to the government of England. In 1719, they had relinquished South Carolina to the British Crown. North Carolina had not brought them the profits for which they had hoped. Instead, it had been a constant source of irritating trouble and complaint.

The monarchy had also become disenchanted with the proprietors and their efforts to govern. In fact, the Crown took over control of a number of its chartered American colonies because they had not added substantially to the royal revenue or adhered to England's mandates, especially its trade laws. In January 1728, seven of the eight proprietors offered to sell their shares to the government of King George II. Only one, John Carteret, Earl Granville, a descendant of the original proprietor Sir George Carteret, retained his share, which became known as the Granville District (see chapter 5). England paid the seven proprietors £2,500 each for their holdings and a lump sum of £5,000 to cover fees and quitrents that the proprietors said were still owed to them. On July 29, 1729, North Carolina became a royal colony, directly subordinate to the king and Parliament in England.

5

A ROYAL COLONY

*W*ith the transfer of North Carolina from the proprietors to the royal government, the colony entered a period of more than four decades of growth and development. Its population increased substantially. Agriculture, industry and trade expanded. Social life, living conditions, learning and contact with the outer world improved. The colony also experienced international war, sectional discord, an internal rebellion and persistent conflict with the king's government in London.

In 1730, North Carolina had a population of about 35,000, including 6,000 enslaved Blacks. By 1775, the population had grown to approximately 345,000, of whom 80,000 were enslaved. Prior to 1730, most of North Carolina's colonists, largely confined to the coastal plain, were English and African, with a small number of Germans, Swiss and French Huguenots. But during the royal era, large numbers of Highland Scots, Scots-Irish and Germans and a few Welsh immigrants arrived in North Carolina. The ever-growing farms and communities of these new immigrants, who began arriving in the 1730s, drove the frontier into the western backcountry. From 1730 to 1775, twenty-six new counties were formed in North Carolina and pushed as far inland as the western edge of the Piedmont.

The Highland Scots' migration into southeastern North Carolina along the Cape Fear River began in 1732, when James Innes of Caithness in the Highlands of Scotland received hundreds of acres in what became Bladen County in 1734. In the next year, Hugh Campbell and William Forbes also received large grants. According to historians Hugh T. Lefler and William S. Powell, "These three

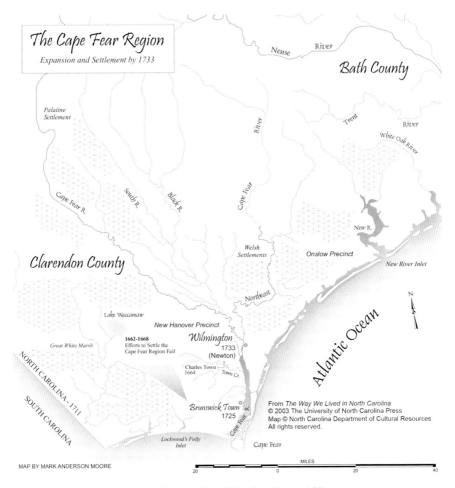

The Cape Fear Region
Expansion and Settlement by 1733

Bath County

Neuse River

Palatine Settlement

Trent River

White Oak River

Cape Fear R.

South R.

Black R.

Cape Fear

River

New R.

Welsh Settlements

Onslow Precinct

New River Inlet

Clarendon County

Lake Waccamaw

Northeast

New Hanover Precinct

Great White Marsh

1662-1668
Efforts to Settle the
Cape Fear Region Fail

Wilmington
1733
(Newton)

NORTH CAROLINA - 1711

SOUTH CAROLINA

Charles Town
1664

Town Cr.

Atlantic Ocean

N

Brunswick Town
1725

From *The Way We Lived in North Carolina*
© 2003 The University of North Carolina Press
Map © North Carolina Department of Cultural Resources
All rights reserved.

Lockwood's Folly
Inlet

Cape Fear

Cape Fear R.

MILES
20   0   20   40

MAP BY MARK ANDERSON MOORE

Map of the Cape Fear region. *North Carolina Office of Archives and History.*

men were the vanguard…of Highland Scots who were to fill up the Cape Fear Valley during the next forty years." A number of factors led the Highlanders to migrate to North Carolina. Most were poor and living under primitive conditions in Scotland. They suffered from a shortage of land and an economic depression at the same time that their population was growing. Their difficulties were compounded when Highland uprisings against the English Crown failed, particularly after the major defeat by England's Duke of Cumberland at the Battle of Culloden in 1746. As a result, many of the clans were broken up, and English landlords took over, charged rents and converted traditional agricultural acreage into fields for sheep grazing. After the defeat of the Scottish rebels at Culloden, King George II offered pardons to all of them who would swear loyalty to the Crown and immigrate to America. Under those circumstances, many Highlanders were lured into making the difficult Atlantic voyage to North Carolina's Cape Fear region with the possibility of owning land, profiting from agricultural crops and forest products then in demand and achieving a higher standard of living.

Over time, thousands of Scots poured into North Carolina through the port of Brunswick. When Wilmington was established in 1733, it became competition for the town of Brunswick for habitation and the import/export trade of the colony and would ultimately supplant Brunswick. The Highlanders pushed their settlements one hundred miles inland from Wilmington in an area that included the present-day counties of Anson, Bladen, Cumberland, Harnett, Hoke, Moore, Richmond, Robeson, Sampson and Scotland. In 1754, the colonial assembly formed Cumberland County out of Bladen. The name of the new county was ironic considering that it derived from the Duke of Cumberland, the "Butcher" who had ordered the slaughter of so many Scots at Culloden. At the headwaters of Cape Fear in Cumberland County in 1762, the town of Campbellton was established. Subsequently, it united with another nearby trading center called Cross Creek, and the two combined sites became known as the town of Cross Creek. After the American Revolution, the community was renamed Fayetteville, after the Marquis de Lafayette of France, who had fought with the Americans in the war.

The Highland Scots became productive Carolinians as farmers, producers of naval stores from the colony's forests of longleaf pines, merchants, artisans and professionals. For a time, many of them continued to speak their native Gaelic, but English eventually surpassed it in usage. In religion, they were largely Presbyterian. During the American Revolution, numbers remained loyal to Britain.

At around the same time that the Highland Scots were inhabiting the Cape Fear region, two other groups from across the Atlantic were arriving in North Carolina—the Scots-Irish (also known as Ulster Scots) and Germans. The history of the Scots-Irish in the colony began after Elizabeth I died in 1603 and the Stuart King James VI of Scotland became King James I of England and began to rule over all of Britain, which then included England, Scotland, Wales and Ireland. James immediately had to deal with trouble from his Irish Catholic subjects, who persisted in their long defiance of English dominance. Historians H. Tyler Blethen and Curtis W. Wood Jr. have written that "James believed that the unruly, 'savage,' Gaelic-speaking Irish could be brought under control and civilized if a Protestant, English-

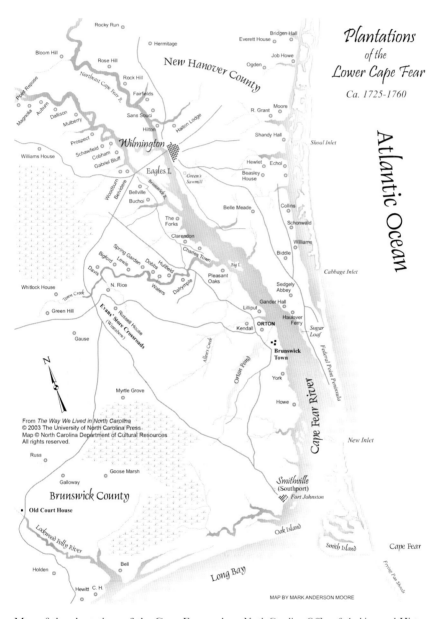

Map of the plantations of the Cape Fear region. *North Carolina Office of Archives and History.*

speaking and politically loyal population was 'planted' in their midst." He therefore began settling Scots from the lowlands of Scotland, who were Presbyterian, and some English, who were Anglican, in Ulster in the northern part of Ireland. By 1715, the lowland Scots made up as much as one-third of the six hundred thousand people living in Ulster. As their numbers continued to grow, they "found themselves living in a hostile environment, and an extraordinarily complex society drawing upon three conflicting but intermingling traditions—Irish, Scottish and English—evolved." The Irish Catholics hated these Scots and the English Anglicans who attempted to rule over them. Religious conflict and an ever-expanding population, combined with a scarcity of land, famine and the rents and restrictions of the landlord-tenant system, led many of the Ulster Scots to emigrate from Ireland to North America, where new opportunities beckoned to them.

Some Scots-Irish appeared in virtually all the British colonies, but the largest number landed in Pennsylvania, disembarking at the port of Philadelphia. Attracted by that colony's progressive political, economic and religious characteristics, they quickly filled its interior. As the population grew and land prices and rents climbed, new generations began to look southward for available and affordable land. By the mid-1730s, they were venturing into the Piedmont of North Carolina. The route over which they traveled was known as the Great Wagon Road. It ran from Philadelphia to Savannah, Georgia, passing through Virginia's Shenandoah Valley and the Blue Ridge Mountains before entering the North Carolina Piedmont, where thousands of Scots-Irish stopped, purchased land and began farming. Like the Highland Scots, they were Presbyterian. But unlike the Highlanders, they harbored no affection or loyalty to the king, and they would eventually compose a large part of the force that fought for independence in the American Revolution. Between 1746 and 1762, the assembly established six counties to absorb and govern the expanding population—Johnston and Granville (1746), Anson (1750), Orange (1752), Rowan (1753) and Mecklenburg (1762). After the war, the Scots-Irish would press on into the mountains of North Carolina.

Large numbers of Germans, too, became part of the influx of immigrants who came down the Great Wagon Road to North Carolina. Political and religious conflict, as well as economic problems, had forced thousands to flee their native land. So many migrated to Pennsylvania by 1775 that one-third of that colony's population was German. At times, these people have been referred to incorrectly as Pennsylvania Dutch. A sizable group had arrived in Piedmont North Carolina by 1747. As with the Scots, available land and economic opportunity were incentives for those migrating southward. The hope of establishing independent communities with a strong religious influence was also a factor. The three German Protestant denominations were Lutheran, German Reformed and Moravian. Lutheran and German Reformed settlers scattered throughout

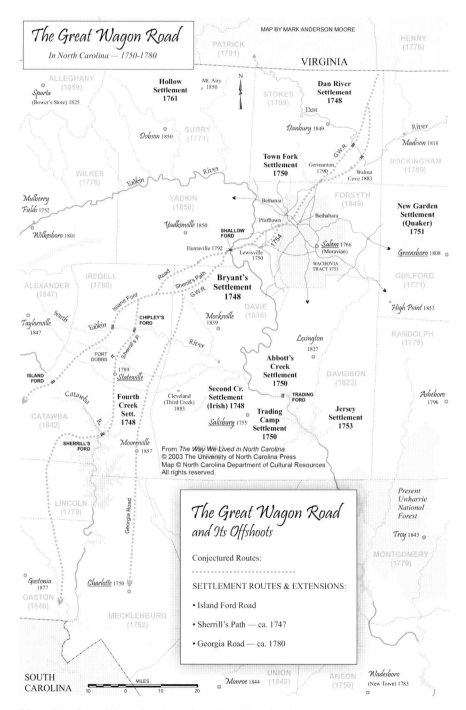

Map of the Great Wagon Road. *North Carolina Office of Archives and History.*

the backcountry. More closely tied together in their unique communities were the Moravians, also known as the United Brethren.

The Moravians were pacifists and had fled Europe to escape religious wars and find religious freedom. Some settled in Georgia as well as Pennsylvania. Their settlement in Georgia did not survive. But the one in Pennsylvania endured, and from there, the Moravians sought a new, expanded location in North Carolina. After investigating the colony from the coast to the foothills of the mountains, Bishop August Gottlieb Spangenberg purchased a 98,985-acre tract in present-day Forsyth County, which was located in the Granville District still owned by Lord Granville. The Moravians paid Granville £500 for the tract, which Spangenberg named Wachovia. The name means "meadowland" or "meadow valley" and probably derives from the German words *wachau* and *aue*, meaning "meadow" and "land," respectively. Apparently, Spangenberg thought Wachovia resembled a valley in Austria that was owned by the Zinzendorf family, Moravian leaders in Europe.

The first Moravians arrived in Wachovia in November 1753 and established the town of Bethabara in that year. The town of Bethania followed in 1759 and Salem in 1766. During the colonial period, the Moravians tended to remain apart from other settlements in order to maintain their own economic, social and religious practices and beliefs and segregate themselves from "worldly influences." Although they hoped to profit from trade, they gave priority to their spiritual and community obligations. Some profits from their businesses went toward public needs and services. The Moravians were craftsmen and merchants, as well as excellent farmers. They and other Germans were less likely to enslave people, preferring to be their own source of labor.

The small number of Welsh who migrated into North Carolina from Pennsylvania planted themselves along tributaries of the Cape Fear River. The area in which they settled was called the Welsh Tract, which, today, is located mostly in Pender County. They were attracted to the region by economic opportunities in the naval stores produced from the area's prolific longleaf pine forests. The first Welshman known to acquire land in the tract was David Evans in 1731. In 1740, Malatiah Hamilton laid out the community of South Washington (incorporated in 1791) at a site where Washington Creek flowed into the northeast Cape Fear River. (South Washington would later be supplanted by the nearby town of Watha, a title derived from the name *Hiawatha*.)

In contrast to the White immigrants, those Black Americans who immigrated to North Carolina did not come willingly. They arrived as enslaved people, first transported to the New World from Guinea in West Africa by European slave traders, who acquired them from African kings who had taken them captive in tribal wars. Most enslaved people who entered North Carolina came from South Carolina and Virginia, but some arrived directly from overseas. The voyage across the Atlantic to the West Indies and mainland America took place under the horrible conditions of the Middle Passage, whereby the Africans were crowded below the decks of slave ships, and many died en route.

Slavery had appeared early in Carolina as a legal system under which enslaved people had no rights. Native slavery existed as late as 1715 but was soon replaced by African slavery. The lords proprietors' Fundamental Constitutions gave the slaveholder "absolute power and authority over his Negro Slaves." During the proprietary period, slaveholding had remained a relatively limited practice in North Carolina, especially when compared to slavery in South Carolina and Virginia. In 1705, the enslaved population of North Carolina totaled nearly one thousand. In the royal era, however, that population climbed substantially and spread throughout the colony. Prior to 1730, the largest concentration of enslaved people worked in the tobacco fields of the Albemarle region, where, in 1700, maybe as many as four hundred slaves lived and labored. In the entire colony, by 1730, that number had increased to about six thousand. It rose to approximately nineteen thousand by 1755 and to more than eighty thousand twenty years later. The greatest number of enslaved people lived east of the fall line. Many worked in the fields and the naval stores industry. Some became craftsmen and mechanics. But all were subject to the strictures and cruelty of enforced servitude. Beginning around 1740, there was an influx of slaves into the rice-growing region of the lower Cape Fear, where the labor was especially hard. The diarist Janet Schaw noted in 1775, "The labor required for the collection [of rice] is fit only for slaves and I think the hardest work I have seen them engage in." According to one source, the average price of an enslaved person varied from £15 to £26, although some were sold for much more, depending on their age, gender and condition and the demand for labor. In 1745, one "prime field hand" was sold for £250.

Not all Black people in North Carolina were enslaved. Free Black people made up about 4.6 percent of the Black population. That percentage varied according to location. In the lower Cape Fear area, where slavery was most dominant, free "persons of color" composed only about 1.5 percent of the

Black population. In the western counties, where slavery was less prevalent, the figure reached 11.6 percent. In addition to enslaved and free Black people, there were a number of Black indentured servants who became free when their indentures expired. Most free Blacks gained their freedom through legal manumission. A few may have arrived in the colony already free or were the children of a Black slave and a White woman. Such mixed-race offspring were free because they were always given the legal status of their mother. Interracial marriage was illegal but sometimes took place. Miscegenation, or sexual relations between White men and enslaved women, was common. Diarist Janet Schaw observed that White slave owners frequently "honour their black wenches with their attention," sometimes "by no other desire or motive but that of adding to the number of slaves." A child born of such a relationship—which was not necessarily consensual—would have been enslaved, because, as noted, offspring had the same legal status as the mother. It is not certain whether free Black people voted in the colonial era, but there was no specific law prohibiting them from doing so. (The Constitution of North Carolina of 1776 allowed free Black people to vote, which they did until they were disenfranchised in 1835.) Over time, the number of free Blacks in North Carolina increased along with that of enslaved African Americans.

Meanwhile, the Indian population in North Carolina continued to decline, as many tribes became indistinct and their members either died or were acculturated into White society. In December 1761, Governor Arthur Dobbs reported that in the eastern colony, the "only remaining Tribes or remains of Tribes" were the "Tuskerora Sapona Meherin and Maramuskito Natives. The Tuskerora have about one hundred fighting men the Sponas and Meherin Natives about twenty each and Maramuskitos about seven or eight." They resided "near Roanoak and have by Law ten thousand acres of Land allotted to them in Lord Granville's District. They live chiefly by hunting and are in perfect friendship with the Inhabitants." He said that in the Piedmont, the Catawba recently had "about three hundred fighting men, but last year, the small pox ravaged their towns, which made them desert them and leave their sick behind them to perish." The Catawba's King Haglar told the governor that they had been "reduced to sixty fighting men and about as many old men and boys and a suitable number of women." In the mountains, the Cherokee "were lately esteemed to be a powerful Tribe and to consist of about three thousand fighting men; they are now upon account of the War Sickness and famine supposed to be reduced to about two thousand." "War Sickness" referred to the Cherokee attack on the western frontier and the Indians' ultimate defeat by a combined North Carolina, Virginia and South Carolina militia, which will be discussed later in this chapter.

As the White and Black populations grew in North Carolina, so did the duties and responsibilities of the royal government in the colony. The structure of the colonial government remained virtually what it had been during the proprietary period. The governor, council, assembly and courts operated as before. Now, though, the king and privy council appointed the governor and some officials, developed trade, enacted new policies and heard the complaints of the colonists, usually presented by the assembly's agent residing in England. The royal government brought more stability and better administration and law enforcement into North Carolina. The royal government also emphasized the mercantile system, whereby its colonies' export-and-import trade helped maintain its imperial defense and standing in the world. This produced closer ties between the colonists and government offices in England, such as the privy council and the board of trade.

But at times, relations between the royal government, represented by the governor, and North Carolinians became heated, as the assembly and governor clashed over such issues as taxes, currency, land distribution and rents, judicial appointments, legislative authority and the rights of the people. In general, the governors were honest and brought more experience and leadership into North Carolina than had existed under the proprietors. But the assembly paid the governor's salary and did not hesitate to withhold it if he attempted to enact measures with which the representatives disagreed. This often placed the governor in the difficult position of having to please both the government in England and the assembly at home. On the other hand, the governor had the power to adjourn the assembly if he disapproved of its efforts, which angered its members, who, as the people's representatives, saw individual rights in the political process being usurped. During the royal period, the colonial government convened in Bath, Edenton, New Bern and Wilmington. In 1766, New Bern was made the colony's permanent capital, and the Governor's Palace, the residence of Governor William Tryon, was constructed there in 1770.

The first royal governor of North Carolina was George Burrington, who had also been governor under the proprietors. He did not get off to a good start when he immediately clashed with the assembly and council over taxes and land policies, and he remained cantankerous and stubborn throughout his term. He disbanded the assembly three times during his years in office (1731–34). He complained, "The Inhabitants of North Carolina…allways behaved insolently to their Governours....All the Governours that ever were in this Province lived in fear of the people (except myself) and Dreaded their Assemblys. The People are neither to be cajoled or outwitted, whenever a Governour attempts to affect anything by these means, he will loose his Labour and show his Ignorance."

The next governor, Gabriel Johnston, performed much better when dealing with the people and their representatives, and his tenure of eighteen years (1734–52) was the longest of any of the royal governors. A well-educated Scot and a former teacher at the University of Saint Andrews, Johnston encouraged and assisted the immigration of Highland Scots into North Carolina and lent considerable support to Wilmington's development. During his years in office, the population of North Carolina grew from thirty thousand to ninety thousand. Johnston proposed revisions to laws and introduced a printing press to the colony. He encouraged new crops and a greater production of pork and corn. Although his leadership was a vast improvement over that of his predecessor, the assembly grew defiant in its dealings with him and the government in England. The two factions were frequently at odds over governmental authority. On occasions, Johnston, too, dissolved the assembly, and Parliament overruled the proposed policies of the colonial legislators. In retaliation and to assert its right to rule, the assembly withheld Johnston's salary for years.

A major problem Johnston had to grapple with was sectional conflict between the northern and southern counties, a dispute that had arisen as early as the Cary Rebellion in the proprietary period. For a long time, the Albemarle region had the most political power, because each of its counties had five delegates in the assembly. The counties in the southern part of the colony, however, had only two delegates per county. Consequently, the northern portion of North Carolina dominated the assembly.

In an effort to correct this inequity, Governor Johnston convened the assembly at Wilmington in 1746. No delegates from the Albemarle region attended, and those present from the southern counties voted to reduce the number of delegates in each northern county to two and proclaimed that New Bern should be made the colony's capital. Incensed at this action, the Albemarle delegates denounced the assembly for its "treachery" and "fraud." At the next session, Albemarle dispatched its customary five delegates, but the assembly refused to seat them. Tempers boiled, and the Albemarle area threatened revolt. But calm prevailed, and both factions called on the royal government to decide the argument over sectional representation. Governor Johnston refused to call for a new election until the disagreement was settled.

In the meantime, many people throughout the colony refused to pay taxes, enforce laws or attend the assembly. Ultimately, in 1754, the royal government ruled for the Albemarle region, which was allowed to keep five delegates for each of its counties. That decision, for a time at least, quieted the sectional argument over representation. But sectional disputes over political power would revive in the future, and the next time, the conflict would be between the eastern and western counties and would bring on armed rebellion.

Dissension over land policies and taxes also arose between the colonists and the royal authorities, including the governor. Colonists could obtain land in North Carolina in different ways. One way, of course, was to purchase it from the British government. When purchasing a tract, the buyer had to pay a fee for the transaction and, in the future, remit an annual tax known as a quitrent to the government. Some inhabitants rented land from the government. Settlers could also acquire land through the "head right" system. In that method, the British Crown granted land to a colonist according to the number of people, including enslaved people, in his family. Usually, the head of the household received one hundred acres, and each member of his family received fifty acres. Land fees, taxes and head rights, which had also existed under the proprietors, continued through the royal period, although, by 1752, head right transactions had ended.

The colonists objected to these high fees, quitrents and land rentals, and they wanted to pay in commodities and "proclamation money," or paper currency, issued by the assembly. The privy council, however, demanded payment in specie, a hard currency of silver or gold, which was in short supply in the colony. North Carolinians also objected to having to pay a poll tax. The assembly insisted that it should decide how taxes were raised and spent. Parliament, just as stubbornly, remained adamant that it was the ultimate authority. Governor Johnston, at times, attempted to mediate between the two, including expressing a willingness to accept commodities and proclamation money for taxes. But in the end, the royal government won out, and Johnston and future governors had to enforce its policies.

As noted previously, when the proprietors relinquished North Carolina to the British government in 1729, one of them, John Carteret, Earl Granville, retained his share of the province. After a number of surveys, the Granville District ran from the coast to the mountains in the upper half of the colony, with the Virginia border as its northern boundary. In 1748, Lord Granville opened a land office in the district and hired land agents to sell tracts, which generally consisted of three hundred to five hundred acres. Granville remained in England, and he had no position or authority in the colonial government. Many settlers took advantage of the low prices and quitrents to purchase land and move into the district. From the time the land office opened until it closed in 1763, it sold nearly two million acres. There were, however, persistent problems with sales, rents and titles. Some land agents proved to be corrupt or inefficient in assigning titles and collecting fees and rents. It was not always clear who owned what property, and conflict arose involving settlers, agents and the governor, council and assembly. Governor Johnston led the attempt to prevent agents' malfeasance, correct discrepancies and reconcile differences. Granville's chief agent, Francis Corbin, came under investigation by the colonial government, and Granville replaced him with Thomas Child. Although the land office closed with the death of Granville in 1763, quarrels over land ownership and revenue continued until the American Revolution, when the state took over the administration of the district. Following the war, the Granville heirs tried to reclaim the property, but a United States court ruled against them.

In addition to dealing with the difficulties in the Granville District, Governor Johnston attempted to resolve a boundary dispute between North Carolina and South Carolina. He and Governor Robert Johnson of South Carolina appointed commissioners to work together to survey a clear boundary line between the two colonies. The surveys of 1735 and 1737 quieted, for a time, the boundary argument but did not resolve it. Future surveys extending westward would be conducted before a final agreement was reached. Gabriel Johnston died in 1752, and Nathaniel Rice and Matthew Rowan, presidents of the council, served consecutively as the temporary chief executive until the next appointed governor, Arthur Dobbs, arrived in North Carolina in 1754.

Dobbs was born in Scotland in 1689, but his family home was Castle Dobbs in County Antrim, Ireland, and he lived there for most of his life. It is not certain where he received his formal education, but his career reveals that he was a man of learning and talent. He served in the British army, managed estates in Ireland and served the Irish government as a surveyor general, high sheriff of Antrim and a member of Parliament. Dobbs possessed a keen interest in science, especially geography, including the possible discovery of a Northwest Passage. He published a number of essays on geography and astronomy and a book on the economy of Ireland, and he prepared an unpublished manuscript on how to thwart the counterfeiting of Irish and English coins. After he settled on an estate near Brunswick in 1758, Dobbs produced "An Account of North Carolina." In correspondence between 1759 and 1760 with English botanist Peter

John Carteret,
Earl Granville.
*State Archives of
North Carolina.*

Collinson, he wrote the earliest recorded descriptions of the Venus flytrap, a rare carnivorous plant that grows only in southeastern North Carolina and a small area of northeastern South Carolina. The seventy-three-year-old Dobbs created some public excitement when he married his second wife, fifteen-year-old Justina Davis. Months later, he suffered a stroke, but he survived and, confined to a wheelchair, remained as governor until he died in 1765.

Dobbs purchased thousands of acres of land in North Carolina, much of which was located in present-day Mecklenburg and Cabarrus Counties, and he invested in the Ohio Company of Virginia, an enterprise for developing the Ohio River Valley. He actively encouraged and recruited Scots-Irish and Europeans to emigrate to the North Carolina backcountry. He proved to

Governor
Arthur Dobbs.
*State Archives of
North Carolina.*

be effective as governor, although, like Johnston, he had his challenges in dealing with the north-south sectional controversy and surveying a boundary line acceptable to both North Carolina and South Carolina. He attempted to help alleviate the tension between the northern and southern counties by establishing a capital at Kingston, renamed Kinston after the Revolution, in present-day Lenoir County. That county was originally part of Dobbs County, formed in 1758 and named in honor of him. Dobbs agreed to sell the land for Kingston at cost, and the assembly appropriated the money. The British government, however, rejected the plan.

Dobbs had the challenge of leading North Carolina during the 1754–63 French and Indian War, as the conflict was called in the North American colonies. It was known internationally as the Seven Years' War. Dobbs arrived in North Carolina the same year the war began, well aware of what the threat of French expansion from Canada southward into the Ohio and Mississippi River Valleys meant for Britain's development and expansion of its North American colonies.

Leading up to the French and Indian conflict, since 1689, competition for dominance on the world stage had brought on four wars between Britain and France, with Spain as an ally of France. The wars were King William's War (or the War of the League of Augsburg, 1689–97); Queen Anne's War (or the War of the Spanish Succession, 1702–13); the War of Jenkins's Ear (between Britain and Spain, 1739–42); and King George's War (or the War of the Austrian Succession, 1740–48). These wars were fought on the continent of Europe and on the high seas, with attacks and raids on the North American colonies. In King William's War, little fighting occurred in the colonies, and none occurred in North Carolina. During Queen Anne's War, both the French and the Spanish "landed and plundered" sites on the coast of North Carolina. In the War of Jenkins's Ear, four hundred North Carolinians, led by Captain James Innes, joined with British regulars in a failed assault on the Spanish town of Cartagena on the coast of Colombia. Only one hundred of the North Carolina troops survived the expedition. The War of Jenkins's Ear evolved into King George's War as the French joined the Spanish against Britain. During that conflict, the Spanish captured at least a dozen North Carolina vessels and raided the towns of Beaufort and Brunswick.

The Anglo-French struggle for a dominant empire—as manifested in those four wars—ultimately erupted into the French and Indian War. The circumstance that ignited the war was the colonial expansion of both Britain and France in North America. Both sides had Indians as allies, although France relied on Native Americans the most. The trouble began when French troops from Canada attempted to secure the Ohio River Valley by establishing a string of forts in the territory. The British colonials, however, claimed that region for their future settlement and land speculation. Both Britain and France considered the valley to be the "gateway to the west" and the key to control over the continent. In 1753, the British government dispatched a letter to the colonial governors, including Dobbs, instructing them "not to take the offensive, but if the enemy invades the undoubted limits of British territory, you must repel force by force."

To inhibit the French advancement southward, Governor Robert Dinwiddie of Virginia, in February 1754, ordered a contingent of militia to march northwestward and establish a fort at the confluence of the Ohio, Allegheny and Monongahela Rivers, the location of present-day Pittsburgh, Pennsylvania. Before the Virginia expedition got underway, however, the French occupied the site and built their Fort Duquesne. Virginia then commanded Major George Washington and 150 militiamen to advance and dislodge them. On May 28, Washington's force defeated a French patrol at Great Meadows, where he constructed Fort Necessity. But there, he and his men were soon overwhelmed by the French and their Native allies and retreated back to Virginia. Those skirmishes signaled the beginning of the war in North America.

Meanwhile, in the summer of 1754, representatives of seven British colonies, with none from North Carolina, met at the Albany Congress in Albany, New York, to coordinate plans against the French. They adopted the "Plan of Union," proposed by Benjamin Franklin. That plan called for a union of the colonies governed by a president general appointed by the British government and a grand council elected by the colonial assemblies. The plan was never enacted, because both the assemblies and the British Crown rejected it.

By this time, however, the government in London had come to realize that the French incursion must be stopped in North America. It sent an army to America to combine with the colonial militia for major military operations against the French. General Edward Braddock arrived in Virginia in April 1755 with 1,400 British regulars, which were supplemented with 450 militia under the command of Major George Washington. Among the militia were about 100 men from North Carolina led by Edward Brice Dobbs, the son of Governor Dobbs. Once assembled, Braddock's force advanced into Pennsylvania to capture Fort Duquesne. On the banks of the Monongahela River in July, they encountered a force of 900 French soldiers and Indians and were nearly annihilated at the Battle of the Wilderness. The North Carolina troops did not take part in the battle because they were on a scouting mission at the time. Braddock was killed, and Washington led the surviving troops to Fort Cumberland in Maryland, where North Carolina's Colonel James Innes was in charge of the colonial militia stationed there.

After the disaster at Duquesne, Britain had some initial success as the war unfolded in the western provinces of the British colonies of New York, New England and Pennsylvania and in French Canada. In June 1755, Governor William Shirley of Massachusetts, who had replaced Braddock, abandoned plans to attack Fort Niagara when French reinforcements arrived. Fort Niagara stood where the Niagara River flowed into Lake Ontario and ensured French control over access to the lake. Although Shirley failed to carry out his operation, Colonels Robert Monckton and John Winslow,

2,000 New England militia and a few regulars were successful in capturing Fort Beauséjour, Nova Scotia, on June 19. From that point, the British drove the French to their Fortress Louisbourg at Cape Breton on the eastern tip of Nova Scotia. From Nova Scotia, in October, its British governor Colonel Charles Lawrence expelled and dispersed throughout the colonies about 6,000 Acadians, who had French heritage and would not take an oath of allegiance or loyalty to the government in England. The British worried that the Acadians might fight for the French. During the summer of 1755, Sir William Johnson, with 3,500 colonists and 400 Natives, constructed Fort William Henry on the southern tip of Lake George in New York in anticipation of a French attack. In September, they defeated 1,400 French and Indians at the Battle of Lake George.

The Seven Years' War phase of the Anglo-French conflict began in Europe in 1756, when Britain officially declared war on France. On the continent, Britain formed an alliance with Prussia, and France allied with Austria. Spain would later join with France and Austria. As they competed for world dominance, Britain and France clashed on the high seas and on a global scale, as far away as India. For the next two years, the war did not go well for the British in Europe or globally, except in India.

The French were also gaining the upper hand in North America. In May 1756, to command the French army in North America, Louis Joseph, Marquis de Montcalm, arrived in Canada, bringing with him reinforcements. Two months later, his opponent, John Campbell, Earl of Loudoun, arrived to take charge of the British forces. Montcalm quickly captured the British fortifications at Oswego, New York, and then moved on to seize Fort William Henry. After the fort's commander, Colonel George Monro, surrendered, Montcalm allowed him to march the surviving soldiers and families from the fort to the nearby British Fort Edward. But France's Native American allies fell upon Monro's column and massacred many of the men, women and children.

When William Pitt rose to head the British government in 1757, he planned an expanded—nearly total war—campaign to defeat the French and establish a worldwide empire for Britain. He demanded and received from the government greater expenditures to achieve victory in Europe and America. Pitt ordered Loudoun to take Fortress Louisbourg. Loudoun assembled a force at Halifax to assault Louisbourg but called off the attack when a French fleet arrived to protect the fortress. After General James Abercromby replaced Loudoun in command, he led a frontal assault on Fort Ticonderoga in New York on July 8, 1758. But Montcalm's troops, although outnumbered, repelled the British with a withering fire that inflicted many casualties and drove them to retreat.

The tide began to turn for the British and their colonial allies when Generals Jeffrey Amherst and James Wolfe—with nine thousand regulars and five hundred militia, supported by a fleet of forty ships—captured Fortress Louisbourg on July 26. From that position, the British then threatened the French in Quebec. A month later, Colonel John Bradstreet took the supply depot and transfer point of Fort Frontenac, which connected the Saint Lawrence River with French outposts to the south and west. That success also gave Britain control over Lake Ontario.

In November 1758, an expedition under General John Forbes that included militia commanded by Colonel Washington marched toward Fort Duquesne. Three companies of North Carolina militia, commanded by Major Hugh Waddell, were among the colonial troops. As Forbes and his men moved through Pennsylvania, the French decided to abandon the fort rather than risk a fight. The British built their own fort at the site and named it Fort Pitt for William Pitt. Governor Dobbs reported that during the campaign, Waddell "had great honour done him being employed in all reconnoitering parties; and dressed and acted as an Indian; and his Sergeant John Rogers took the only Indian prisoner who gave Mr. Forbes certain intelligence of the Forces in Fort Duquesne upon which they resolved to proceed." The French capitulation at Duquesne meant that the British then held dominance over much of the Ohio River Valley.

At this point, wrote historian Bernard Bailyn, "the iron ring around the northern British colonies had been broken at three critical points: on the east (Louisbourg and Nova Scotia), the west (Frontenac and Lake Ontario) and the south (Duquesne)." Britain had also prevailed in Africa and India. Pitt laid out the plan for the final victory over France in America. The British would take Fort Niagara and cut off Canada from the west. Amherst would drive into Canada from Lake Champlain and the Saint Lawrence River Valley. Wolfe would launch an amphibious attack on Quebec via the Saint Lawrence River.

On July 25, 1759, a contingent of two thousand regulars, commanded by General John Prideaux, and one hundred Indians, led by Sir William Johnson, captured Fort Niagara. Around the same time, the French abandoned and destroyed the forts at Ticonderoga and Crown Point near Lake Champlain. After rebuilding and occupying the forts, Amherst did not have enough time left in the season to start his campaign from the south.

Wolfe, on the other hand, did not hesitate to carry out his part of Pitt's strategy. With a good deal of daring and luck, he managed to transport nearly 10,000 men and two hundred ships up the Saint Lawrence River to the French stronghold at the city of Quebec. He found that taking the city presented a major obstacle. The citadel was located at the top of 150-foot-tall cliffs that composed the shore of the river. He spent some weeks in search of a way to scale the heights and take the heavily fortified city. Finally, he found a route west of the city. On the night of September 12, 1759, he and 4,500 soldiers climbed the cliff and formed for battle on the Plains of Abraham, west of the city. The French charged the well-formed and disciplined British line and came under a deadly fire that devastated their ranks and forced their surrender. The British suffered relatively few casualties, but Wolfe was killed in the battle. The French also lost their commander, Montcalm.

With the French army much depleted after Quebec, Montreal remained the last bastion of French power and authority in Canada. In 1760, Amherst marched northeast from the Great Lakes to Montreal and deployed in front of the city. His force was joined there by a contingent from Quebec. The French realized that further resistance against the British onslaught was futile. On September 8, Pierre François de Regaud, Marquis de Vaudreuil and governor of Canada, surrendered to Britain all of New France (Canada and territory in the Mississippi River Valley).

The Treaty of Paris of 1763 settled the final terms of the surrender. France ceded to Britain possession of all of North America east of the Mississippi River, including Canada and Nova Scotia but excluding New Orleans. Britain allowed France fishing rights off Newfoundland and returned a number of French islands that it had captured in the West Indies. Spain, which had joined the war in 1761 in support of France, had to relinquish East and West Florida to Britain in exchange for the return of Cuba, which the British had captured in 1762. France honored its pledge to Spain for joining its war effort and granted it New Orleans and the land west of the Mississippi River.

The North Carolina militia did not play a large role in major operations against the French, which occurred mostly in the north. The colony's troops participated in both of the expeditions to capture Fort Duquesne and campaigned briefly in New York. After Braddock's crushing defeat, however, they were said to have "deserted in great numbers."

North Carolina devoted most of its war effort to protecting its frontier from Native attacks. In the south, the French allied with various tribes but especially the Creek and the Cherokee. Originally, the Cherokee—who inhabited an area in western North Carolina, South Carolina, Georgia and Virginia—had been friendly with the British. A number of them had accompanied the North Carolina militia on its expedition against Fort Duquesne in 1755. After that disaster—when, on their way home, some of them were killed by White Virginians—the Cherokee changed sides and began raiding the North Carolina frontier. In 1756, the assembly ordered Hugh Waddell to build a fort near present-day Statesville to repel any Cherokee attacks eastward. The fortification was named Fort Dobbs for the governor. By 1759, reports had grown about Cherokee raids and atrocities committed against colonists in the Catawba and Yadkin River Valleys. On February 3, 1760, the Cherokee moved on Fort Dobbs, but Waddell and his men drove them off.

Subsequently, Colonel Archibald Montgomerie, commanding a regiment of 1,600 Highland Scots and several hundred militiamen, led a foray into Cherokee country. In late June 1760, the Cherokee ambushed and defeated his column at Echoee, near present-day Franklin in Macon County. As violence and massacre between White settlers and the Cherokee continued, North Carolina, South Carolina and Virginia launched a joint, all-out campaign against the Cherokee. In June 1761, at a short distance from where the Cherokee had defeated Montgomerie, Colonel James Grant and about 2,600 Highlanders overwhelmed the Cherokee and "drove them into recesses in the mountains, burned their granaries, laid waste their fields and pushed the frontier seventy miles farther west." More land now lay open for future White settlement westward.

After the Treaty of Paris was signed in February 1763, Britain still wanted to negotiate a treaty with the Indians in its southern colonies in order to maintain peace and enable expansion toward the Mississippi River. King George III, therefore, ordered the governors of North Carolina, South Carolina, Georgia and Virginia to reach a peaceful settlement with the Natives. In November 1763, the governors, including Dobbs, met at a conference or congress in Augusta, Georgia, with twenty-five chiefs and seven hundred warriors of the Cherokee, Chickasaw, Creek and Catawba tribes. Also present was John Stuart, Britain's superintendent of Indian affairs in the Southern District. Stuart informed the tribes that the colonies spoke as a united voice for the king and asked them to act as one body also. On November 10, the two sides signed a formal treaty that declared "That a Perfect and perpetual Peace and sincere Friendship shall be continued." It specified that neither side would seek revenge for past attacks or other violence. Colonists would be permitted to trade with the Natives. Both parties agreed to punish any of their people who committed theft or murder against the other side. The Creek Indians gave up almost 2.5 million acres of their territory in Georgia, and the Catawba received only a small reservation in South Carolina. The British agreed not to push onto Native land beyond the boundaries that then existed.

After 1763, with the French and Indian War ended and the Indian threat suppressed for the moment, economic and social life revived in North Carolina. Immigration had been inhibited during the conflict but soon revived, and within two years, the colony's population had grown to two hundred thousand. The backcountry continued to fill as more settlers arrived via the Great Wagon Road.

From its earliest days under the proprietors, North Carolina's economy had been based on agriculture and the small industries connected to the fields and forests. About 95 percent of the colony's population was involved in raising crops, manufacturing naval stores or producing lumber. More prosperous inhabitants often managed to engage in all three at different times of the year. Farmers adopted a number of crops from the Natives, including maize or corn, beans, peas, white potatoes, sweet potatoes and squash. Colonists attempted to introduce some European crops, such as olives and French grapes. Most did not survive, but wheat and oats proved successful.

Tobacco was the colony's largest cash crop and was grown mostly in the Albemarle area, the Roanoke River Valley and the Granville District. Colonial tobacco was of the burley variety (the flue-cured bright-leaf of today came much later) and was air cured or sun cured. Once farmers cured their tobacco, they packed the leaves, which had been inspected by a government official, into round, one-thousand-pound hogsheads (barrels) and transported them to a coastal port for shipment overseas, usually to England.

Corn was probably North Carolina's most prolific crop and was grown throughout the colony. Corn could help feed a family and livestock and could be ground into meal at a water-powered gristmill. It could also be distilled into whiskey. Thousands of bushels of corn shipped out of North Carolina each year. Wheat was primarily a commercial crop grown for export. Farmers in all areas of the state grew it, and it could be ground into flour at water-powered gristmills. Much of the colony's wheat and flour was exported to the West Indies and other colonies. Additional agricultural produce consisted of an assortment of beans, peas and other foodstuffs, some of which were exported. In the lower Cape Fear region, a limited amount of rice and indigo was cultivated. Various fruits and vegetables tended to be produced for home sustenance. As forage for their livestock, farmers grew alfalfa and timothy grass. Although land remained plentiful and cheap, it had to be cleared for agriculture. And the system of farming remained primitive.

Farmers did not practice crop rotation or realize the benefits of using manures as fertilizer. Consequently, much of the land became exhausted. A shortage of good farming tools and equipment frequently made planting and harvesting difficult.

North Carolina farmers raised considerable livestock: cattle, horses, oxen, hogs, sheep, chickens, geese and other fowl. As draft animals, oxen and horses performed heavy work, such as plowing and hauling. Horses also served for riding and transportation. Most livestock animals were left to roam and forage for themselves. Farmers branded their cattle and horses and notched the ears of their razorback swine for identification. North Carolinians had a wide reputation for raising a vast number of hogs. The colonists drove large herds of them overland to Virginia and Pennsylvania for sale and exported large quantities of pork to the West Indies and other markets. Cattle were rounded up in pens and then herded to market in Virginia, South Carolina and Pennsylvania. Some were slaughtered and the salted beef shipped abroad. Sheep provided wool and could also be slaughtered for family consumption.

Little in colonial North Carolina could be called commercial industry. Most manufacturing occurred on a small scale at home. Households generally provided their own food and made their own clothing, much of their furniture, utensils and leather goods from animal hides. Virtually every farmhouse had a spinning wheel and loom from which wool, flax and a bit of cotton could be spun and woven for cloth. The ownership of imported items, such as fashionable clothing and furniture, metal cookware, sugar, tea, coffee, chocolate, silverware, silks, china and other "luxuries," depended on the wealth of the family.

North Carolina's main commercial industry was the production of naval stores, which became the colony's number one export. North Carolina produced more tar, pitch, turpentine and rosin than any other British colony. To derive those products, workers scored pine trees to drain and collect sap, which was then melted, boiled or distilled and stored in barrels for shipment. The industry was largest in the Cape Fear region, where the longleaf pine was most prolific.

A sizable lumber industry also operated during the colonial era. It developed early on a commercial basis, as the demand for wood grew for construction and wooden containers, such as casks, hogsheads and barrels. Water-powered sawmills made boards from the harvested trees. Cooperage, or barrel making, rose as one of North Carolina's most active industries. Naval stores and most other exports were shipped in barrels. Lumber exports consisted of "chiefly barrel staves, headings and hoops of oak; shingles, largely from cypress, and boards, mainly of pine." These were shipped to a number of markets abroad, with more than half going to the West Indies. Some shipbuilding took place in North Carolina, mostly for small vessels, but it did not become a large industry utilizing the colony's lumber.

Other local industries were the water-powered gristmills for grinding corn and wheat and tanneries for producing leather. Artisans manufactured a number of items and provided certain skilled services. These craftsmen and skilled workers included coopers (barrel makers), shoemakers, hatters, tailors, seamstresses, bakers, carpenters, brick and stone masons, cabinetmakers, gunsmiths, silversmiths and blacksmiths. The majority lived and worked in or near urban areas.

Historian Hugh T. Lefler has written, "The colonial merchant was not a specialist. Many of them were both wholesalers and retailers; many were both exporters and importers; some were planter merchants; some…owned and operated shops; a number were money lenders and the main source of credit in their communities." Those merchants who did business on a large scale were located primarily in the towns of the coastal plain: New Bern, Wilmington, Edenton and Cross Creek. But stores of various sizes opened throughout the colony. In the Piedmont, Salem and nearby Bethabara and Bethania became the chief mercantile centers. Other communities, such as Hillsborough, Salisbury and Charlotte, had stores. Merchants wanted to deal only in cash payments, but the lack of specie compelled them to accept produce in payment and to grant credit to customers. In turn, British wholesale merchants allowed them credit and payments with coin or such commodities as naval stores or tobacco.

Transportation and communication in North Carolina remained primitive throughout the colonial period. As noted earlier, the lack of good coastal harbors limited the colony's commercial activity with the outside world. Nevertheless, the export-import commerce of the colony depended heavily on maritime shipping, and some planters and shipping merchants managed sizable profits. Navigable rivers and streams were important modes of travel and trade, and farms and plantations tended to be located nearby. Flat-bottom scows and large canoes transported goods and livestock downstream to markets and ports.

The colony's roads were few and generally in poor condition. Construction and maintenance were irregular and inefficient. The assembly and county governments devoted little attention or expense to them. Diarist Janet Schaw observed that "the only making they bestow upon the roads in the flat part of the country is cutting down the trees…in as even a line as they can, and where the ground is wet, they make a small ditch on either side." Holes, fallen limbs and trees, river and creek crossings and washouts often made travel difficult and even hazardous. Some of the earliest roads were derived from former Native trading paths. Several roads ran south from Virginia to South Carolina. One of these was a route through Edenton, Bath, Wilmington and Brunswick. Another traversed from Halifax on the Roanoke River to Tarboro on the Tar-Pamlico River. One route tied Cross Creek on the Cape Fear River to communities to the north. The building of roads from east to west came last due to the Piedmont's large trade with Virginia and South Carolina, as well as the difficulty of constructing roads across rivers flowing from north to south. But the old, long, winding "Great Trading Path" connected the coastal plain to the mountains. A variety of vehicles rolled over the roads. Two-wheeled carts could carry as much as one thousand pounds and four-wheeled wagons as much as two thousand pounds. Carriages, gigs and other private "pleasure vehicles," as well as riders on horseback, used the roads. Pedestrians walked long distances from place to place along the same routes. Commercial stagecoaches would not be introduced in North Carolina until well after the American Revolution.

As much as bad roads, a shortage and the poor quality of bridges and ferries hindered trade and commerce. Counties contracted with individuals to build bridges and used taxes to pay for them. Some counties allowed private parties to construct them at their own expense and to charge a toll. Ferries brought better results than bridges. Both the assembly and county courts authorized ferries. According to historian Alan D. Watson, "When authorizing ferry service, the courts determined the location of the ferry, the boats required for transport, rates charged for service and bonds for ensuring the proper performance of duties by ferry keepers." He concluded, "By the end of the colonial period, North Carolina probably possessed a sufficient number of ferries for its transportation network, though the quality of ferriage service may have been questionable."

The colony attempted to establish a postal service, but it never became more than slow and erratic. Originally, government dispatches were carried out to towns and plantations by messengers on horseback. Private letters were sent by riders paid by the correspondents. In the 1750s, the colony negotiated contracts with James Davis, its first public printer and newspaper publisher, to dispatch post riders every fifteen days to Virginia with official communications and to return with that government's proceedings. At the outbreak of the American Revolution, however, North Carolina still did not have an effective mail service. The only postal route in the colony went through Edenton, Bath, New Bern and Wilmington, and those towns had postmasters.

Yet by that time, North Carolina's economy and communities had grown significantly, even if they had grown more slowly and less dramatically than those of other British colonies. A clear social structure had been defined among its population, even though class distinctions were probably less pronounced in North Carolina than they were in Virginia and South Carolina. Alan D. Watson writes, "The seemingly endless influx of immigrants and their servants and slaves re-created the stratified societies of Europe. Although the English mainland colonies in general, and North Carolina in particular, seemed quite democratic by eighteenth-century standards, society was nevertheless structured into a hierarchy of classes."

At the top of the social scale ranked the gentry, which consisted of planters, government officials, large shipping merchants and some professionals, such as lawyers and clergy. Their wealth in land, enslaved people and commerce, as well as their education, gained them their upper-class status. Although they made up the smallest percentage of the population, they wielded the most political power and influence in society. A number had ties to the gentry back in Britain.

Women who were fortunate enough to be members of the gentry, like those below them in social standing, had to endure a second-class existence tied largely to their husbands, families and households. Once a woman was married, all her real and personal property became the property of her husband, and she had few legal options. But unmarried women and widows had legal rights that were denied to married women. According to authorities Margaret Supplee Smith and Emily Herring Wilson, "They could buy and sell property, make wills and contracts, sue in court, execute deeds, administer estates and serve as guardians. They could not sit on juries, serve as government officials, or hold office in local councils or courts." Whether married or single, women could not vote in political elections. Divorce was difficult and had to be approved by the assembly.

Despite their disadvantages, women played strong roles in colonial society. They supervised the work on plantations and farms, ran businesses—owned by their husbands or male relatives, or, if single, by themselves—and defended their own interests as best they could amid circumstances that discriminated against them. In the proprietary period, some women served as lawyers in legal transactions and court proceedings. One such woman was Ann Marwood Durant, the wife of George Durant, in the Albemarle region. She was the "first attorney-in-fact on record in North Carolina."

The mother of nine children, she, with her husband, operated an inn in the Perquimans Precinct, where the colonial assembly and court often met. She represented her own and her husband's interests and those of other clients in the court proceedings held at the inn. In one case, for example, she successfully brought forward a suit to retrieve lost wages for a sailor, Andrew Ball. Another woman who acted as a de facto attorney was Juliana Hudson Taylor Laker, the "longest female participant in the colonial courts." She "pursued her legal interests, protecting her property rights and defending herself against charges of 'unreasonable correctings,' with determination, competence and occasional vindictiveness for almost fifty years." But, write Smith and Wilson, "when courts became more formal and structured at the close of the proprietary period, women lost out…and male professional attorneys were in charge."

The middle class made up the largest portion of North Carolina's population. It contained yeomen (small, largely self-sufficient farmers), small merchants and artisans. Many free Black people who were landowning farmers and artisans qualified as middle class, even when White society did not recognize them as equals. Closely associated with the middle class were indentured servants and apprentices. Apprentices were youth bound by law to work for an artisan for a certain number of years—usually until the age of twenty-one for boys and eighteen for girls. In exchange for their services and obligations to their master or mistress, they were taught a skill or craft. When the indenture or apprenticeship ended, the servants or apprentices were free to embark on their own careers as members of the middle class. At the bottom of the socioeconomic ladder among White colonists were the poorest farmers, laborers and persons without any consistent resources or livelihood. Only enslaved Africans were held in less regard.

The assembly passed laws to control enslaved people and restrict their freedom. Slaves could not leave their plantations without a pass from their master, and a 1753 law created slave patrols to keep track of African Americans' movements. An earlier law made it illegal for a slave to be away from the master's property "Arm'd with any Gun, Sword or any other Weapon of defence." Colonists lived in constant fear that the enslaved population would rise up in violent revolt. Masters could not free their slaves without authorization from county courts. Laws also prohibited the enslaved from voting, marrying White people or holding any sort of gathering, including religious services. Masters frequently whipped their slaves as punishment for perceived bad conduct or infractions of plantation rules. For violation of the law, county courts ordered whipping and the cropping of an enslaved person's ears. A few Black people convicted of murder were sentenced by the courts to burn at the stake.

For most colonial Carolinians, life was a blend of past and present, old and new. When immigrants arrived in the colony, they brought with them from Britain or Europe traditional values, customs and a familiarity with a stratified socioeconomic system. Their religion, music and folkways reflected those of their ancestors across the Atlantic. For a time, some of the earliest settlers—specifically the Germans, French and Welsh—continued to speak their native languages. But those inhabitants of the Old World who made the journey to North Carolina also experienced a new beginning that offered landownership, individual and religious liberty, a political voice and the possibility of moving up the social scale.

Of course, the gentry could afford housing and social and cultural advantages not enjoyed by the classes beneath them. The earliest dwellings in colonial North Carolina were log structures built directly on the ground. Most originally consisted of one room with a fireplace, a dirt floor and a loft. A log shed or outbuilding might stand on the property. Many of those early houses did not survive as permanent homes, as their owners managed to build more substantial dwellings on brick or stone foundations that included additions and second floors. For newcomers and poorer folk, however, logs continued to serve as a common building material throughout the period.

Although the gentry constructed the most sophisticated houses, which provided more privacy, convenience and sanitation, they were not comparable to the grandiose mansions owned by the aristocracy back in England. Most North Carolina dwellings were made of wood and had two stories with rooms, hallways and fireplaces downstairs and upstairs. The outbuildings might have included a laundry, kitchen and office. In the coastal plain, especially, wood dominated. According to architectural historians Catherine W. Bishir and Michael T. Southern, "Confronted with a scarcity of good building stone and high costs for making brick and obtaining lime, eastern North Carolina restricted masonry construction to the very finest houses and public buildings." In the west, as that region developed, brick and stone were more common. Slave quarters were the most incommodious of all housing. Customarily, they were log dwellings, crowded and smoky, with dirt floors and stick-and-mud chimneys, and they were ill insulated against winter weather. Indentured servants and apprentices usually had better accommodations, sometimes living in the house or shop of the person to whom they were bound.

The Newbold-White House (1730), Perquimans County. *State Archives of North Carolina.*

The quality of clothing, furniture and personal and household amenities naturally depended on the wealth of each family. They varied from the homemade items of the lower classes to the luxuries imported from abroad by the gentry. Entertainment could also differ according to social standing. Although there was a distinction in the social order, the upper and lower classes often mingled together at militia musters, court sessions and church services and in taverns and other public venues. But they also engaged in different and separate social activities and recreation.

Farm families in the backcountry convened at such community gatherings as house and barn raisings, corn shuckings, picnics and sporting events, where men participated in "jumping, wrestling, footraces and quoits, a game similar to horseshoes." The wrestling could be vicious. Alan D. Watson writes, "The lower classes engaged in their notorious wrestling matches, in which North Carolinians prided themselves on their ability to scratch, bite, kick and gouge out eyes." Public meetings gave women an opportunity to receive news, have conversation and gain mutual support. At times, they met in individual households to socialize while quilting or spinning.

The Cupola House (1758–59), Edenton, prior to its twentieth-century restoration. *State Archives of North Carolina.*

All classes enjoyed dancing in reels and hops, often to tunes from a fiddle. The gentry, however, also held more sophisticated balls, with the dancers formally attired. They attended refined parties that included elaborate food and drink. Card playing was a favorite party activity. Men of the upper and lower classes attended together the popular cockfights and horse races, where they drank, grew boisterous, placed their bets and cheered on their champions.

Entertainment for the enslaved was limited by the strictures of their bondage, including a prohibition against large gatherings. But they took advantage of their opportunities for socializing. Conversation, the retelling of African folktales, playing music, singing and dancing occurred when possible in the slave cabins. Spiritual songs about religious uplift and the possibility of liberation rendered special comfort and pleasure. By the late colonial era, most enslaved people had embraced Christianity. They often accompanied their masters to church but were prohibited from gathering for services of their own.

Whether wealthy or poor, enslaved or free, all North Carolinians were susceptible to the illnesses and diseases that afflicted colonial society. Those

The Chowan County Courthouse (1767), Edenton. *State Archives of North Carolina.*

who settled in the tidewater were especially—but not exclusively—prone to contract malaria, which was spread by the mosquitoes that thrived in low-lying areas. Other diseases that ran rampant throughout the colony included smallpox, measles, typhoid, typhus, cholera, whooping cough, diphtheria and mumps. Yellow fever, introduced possibly from Africa via the slave trade and spread by mosquitoes, appeared in the port towns. Infant mortality and childhood death rates were high. Many women died in childbirth, and it became common for a man to marry twice or even three times in his lifetime. Enslaved people and poor White people particularly suffered from hookworm and pellagra. Little existed that could be called good medical care by present-day standards. Doctors lacked the formal education of some physicians in Europe. Even if they had such training, medical knowledge worldwide was limited at best. In North Carolina, just about anyone could claim to be a doctor. The practitioners had no awareness of bacteria or viruses and did not recognize the importance of sanitation and the causes of infection. Their treatments usually consisted of dispensing questionable drugs and herbal remedies, primitive surgery and bleeding and purging patients. Inoculations against smallpox were not introduced in North Carolina until the American Revolution, and even then, only in certain areas.

Churches played a significant role in both the spiritual and social lives of North Carolinians under royal rule. The Church of England (or Anglican Church) remained the official church of the colony. The gentry made up most of its membership. The Anglican Saint Thomas Church (1734) in Bath is, today, the oldest surviving church building in North Carolina. Other denominations continued to flourish, including Presbyterian, Baptist, Methodist, Quaker, Moravian, Lutheran and German Reformed. Churches not only provided religious, moral and charitable guidance but also gave people an opportunity to gather for communication and socialization. Churches formed the vanguard for education in North Carolina and the other British colonies, where illiteracy was high and educational opportunities were limited.

Churches established most of the colony's early schools, and their teachers were largely clergy or lay readers. Missionaries of the Society for the Propagation of the Gospel in Foreign Parts were some of the earliest pioneers to become teachers and found the "first parish or public libraries." The colony's first verifiable schoolteacher, Charles Griffin (or Griffith), a lay reader for the Anglican Church, started a school in Pasquotank County. He was said to have done well until James Adams, a missionary for the Society for the Propagation of the Gospel, claimed that he "fell into the sin of fornication and joined with the Quaker interest."

The number of schools in North Carolina remained sparse, and initially, they excited little interest among small farmers, who were preoccupied with making a living from the soil. Significant formal education resided with the members of the upper class, who had their children educated by tutors or at small private academies. For higher education, the gentry sent their children out of the colony, sometimes to England. But as the Scots-Irish and Germans settled in the backcountry, they created a few schools for their offspring. In 1756, the Moravians could claim schoolteachers, a "day school" and a "school for older boys." The colonial assembly passed

Saint Thomas Church (1734), Bath. *State Archives of North Carolina.*

some legislation to establish public, or "free," schools in the counties, but little resulted from those efforts, as the limited funds for the schools were "borrowed and employed" for other purposes. In Mecklenburg County, Presbyterians led a movement to establish the first college in North Carolina. Their efforts resulted in the assembly's passage of an act in January 1771 that incorporated Queens College in Charlotte. The school was initially funded by a tax on rum imported into the county. Although this was disallowed by the British Crown, the college nevertheless continued to operate without a charter until the American Revolution, when the state assembly chartered it as Liberty Hall. It collapsed during the war and reemerged afterward under a new charter as an academy in Salisbury. (The present-day Queens

University of Charlotte—formerly known as Queens College—was founded for female students in 1857.)

As in the realm of formal education, books and libraries were mostly luxuries for the wealthiest North Carolinians. The Society for the Propagation of the Gospel in Foreign Parts shipped a limited number of books into the colony, some of which went to the creation of a "free public library" in Saint Thomas Parish in Beaufort County. The library, however, had little management and few patrons.

A printing press did not arrive in North Carolina until the mid-eighteenth century. Before then, all of the colony's printing had to be done elsewhere. For many years, the colonial government had needed a local press to print the laws passed by the assembly and other documents. Finally, in 1749, the assembly authorized the hiring of a printer with funds from a tax. In June of that year, James Davis, a printer from Williamsburg, Virginia, began operating his press in New Bern, printing the acts of the assembly. He continued to print government documents, as well as books, pamphlets and sermons, for the next thirty-three years. In 1751, he launched the colony's first newspaper, the *North Carolina Gazette*.

The influx of immigrants into the backcountry of North Carolina continued to swell until the 1760s, when more people were living in the western part of the colony than in the eastern counties. Along with that transformation in population, the old problem of sectional and class conflict again arose. This time, the conflict was not—as with the Cary Rebellion in the proprietary era—between the northern and southern regions of the coastal plain but between the old, established eastern province and the new, expanding western area of North Carolina. As before, the clash between the sections was about one region's—in this case, the east's—dominance in the government, because it had the most representatives in the assembly. More counties existed in the east, despite the fact that more people were then living in the west. Having control of the assembly, the eastern power bloc, controlled by the planter aristocracy, formed new counties in such a way as to ensure its political domination. Furthermore, between 1765 and 1771, the governor, members of the council, all judges, the treasurer and the speaker of the house resided in the east. Unrest over this inequity in political power continued to grow in the backcountry.

The disenchantment of the small farmers in the Piedmont was compounded by the undemocratic system of their county governments, wherein no officials were elected by popular vote. Justices of the peace controlled the county courts and the administrative affairs of the counties.

They were appointed by the governor, who was residing in the east. The justices, in turn, appointed or recommended to the governor all the other county officials, including the sheriff, who had to be a former justice. Almost two-thirds of the assembly was composed of the county justices of the peace. This created a political bond that produced the so-called courthouse rings that engendered favoritism and corruption among county officials—sheriffs, judges, registers of deeds, tax collectors, land agents and clerks of court—who could not be voted out of office. Folk in the backcountry maintained that many of those officers were charging high, unfair and even extortionate taxes and fees, embezzling public money and illegally seizing land for themselves. A few of the officials did not even live in the counties in which they served.

Two officials especially despised by the farmers in the Piedmont were Edmund Fanning, an assemblyman, register of deeds, militia commander, judge and land speculator; and Henry Eustace McCulloh, a justice of the peace who also speculated in land. In May 1765, a band of farmers marched on land that McCulloh was having surveyed for himself and George A. Selwyn. The protestors claimed that McCulloh had no legal right to the property and was guilty of selling land at exorbitant prices and trying to evict some of them from their property. He was absent at the time of the protest, but the farmers set upon and beat the six surveyors. McCulloh wrote to Fanning that "had I been present—I most assuredly and without ceremony had been murdered." The mob had "declared solemnly—publicly, they will put me to death."

Responsibility for dealing with the sectional discord festering in the colony fell to the new governor of North Carolina William Tryon, who succeeded Arthur Dobbs. Tryon was born in 1729 to a gentry family at Norbury Park in Surrey, England. At the age of twenty-two, he embarked on a successful career in the British army. In 1757, he married Margaret Wake, for whom North Carolina's Wake County is named. That marriage brought him considerable wealth and connections with Britain's ruling class. Among those connections was one with Wills Hill, Lord Hillsborough, for whom the North Carolina town of Hillsborough is named. It was probably Hillsborough, lord of trade and plantations, who secured for Tryon the position of governor of North Carolina. Tryon arrived in the Cape Fear area in October 1764, with the assignment of replacing Dobbs. The transition was delayed for a time but took place at the time of Dobbs's death in March 1765.

Governor Tryon attempted to bring to justice the "rioters" who had invaded McCulloh's land and attacked the surveyors. He offered to pardon

Edmund Fanning.
*State Archives of
North Carolina.*

"any two" of them who would give up the names of the others. Apparently, no one took him up on the offer. The riot went unpunished by the courts and became remembered as the War of Sugar Creek.

Another protest against abuses by local officials began in June 1765, when George Sims, a schoolmaster in the Nutbush community, delivered "An Address to the People of Granville County," calling for an end to dishonest practices in county governments. The document became known as the Nutbush Address. A mass meeting ensued at Sandy Creek in Orange County, where the delegates issued a document later referred to as Regulator Advertisement Number One, which called on the people to protest actively against corruption among their officials and to hold them accountable. A rising leader of the protest movement, Herman Husband, probably wrote the document. The dissenters issued a number of these "advertisements," or declarations, as they uniformly adopted the title Regulators. The county

The Governor's Palace (1767–70), New Bern. *State Archives of North Carolina.*

officials curtly responded that they were not obliged to respond to any demands of a so-called mob. The citizens of Orange County then asked the assembly to address their concerns, but the assembly ignored their request.

Dissatisfaction grew in the Piedmont when, in 1766, Governor Tryon persuaded the assembly to locate the colony's permanent capital at New Bern and build the Governor's Palace in that town. A new tax to pay for the grand edifice infuriated the backcountry farmers, most of whom would never see the governor or visit the capital in the east. Construction on the palace began in 1767 and was completed in 1770.

Tryon was sympathetic to a degree to the Regulators' complaints, and he acknowledged that half of the taxes collected by the sheriffs could not be accounted for. In December 1757, he called for better control over county offices to prevent corruption and supported the assembly in passing new regulations to prevent the illegal collection of fees by county officials, as well as laws concerning the appointment and regulation of sheriffs and their duties. At the same time, the governor instructed the Regulators to disband, pay their taxes and obey the law.

By the spring of 1768, the number of Regulators had grown, and the grievances of the backcountry folk were still not rectified by the government. Meeting in Orange County in March, they declared that they would remain unified and pay no taxes or fees that were not specifically authorized by law. Around the same time, violence erupted after an Orange County sheriff seized the horse, saddle and bridle of a Regulator as payment for his unpaid taxes. In response, a band of outraged Regulators rode into the county seat of Hillsborough, grabbed their friend's property and fired guns into Edmund Fanning's house. Fanning then formed a company of armed men that rode to Sandy Creek, arrested the Regulators' leaders Herman Husband and William Butler and locked them in the jail in Hillsborough. A group of armed Regulators responded to the arrest by marching to Hillsborough to free the two prisoners. When he heard of the Regulators' approach, the sheriff released Husband and Butler. Upon learning of the trouble in Hillsborough, Governor Tryon ordered that the Regulators disband, lawful taxes be collected and any official engaged in extortion be prosecuted. The Regulators immediately charged Fanning with extortion.

All three individuals—Husband, Butler and Fanning—stood trial at the September 1768 session of the Orange County Superior Court. Tryon led a contingent of militiamen to Hillsborough to protect the court in the event that trouble arose from the large group of Regulators who gathered nearby. Husband and Butler were charged with rioting. The court acquitted Husband but convicted Butler, who, at Tryon's request, received a pardon from the king. Fanning was convicted of extortion but received a sentence of only a small fine, which infuriated the Regulators and increased their distrust of the courts.

Disappointed in the court ruling regarding Fanning and still concerned that their complaints were not being addressed, the Regulators turned again to the governor and the assembly for a peaceful redress of their grievances. When the assembly met in 1769, a number of Regulators had been elected as members. Before their concerns received attention, however, Tryon dissolved the assembly and called for new elections. His reason was not related directly to the Regulators but rather to a dispute between the assembly and the British Parliament over taxation. Before adjourning, the assembly did resolve that any public official who charged illegal taxes and fees would be prosecuted. But little action resulted from that decree, and the Regulators were left once again without effective measures to correct their difficulties in the backcountry.

Still unsatisfied and angry, they grew more restive, and in September 1770, they rioted at the Orange County Superior Court in Hillsborough. They broke up the court, assaulted several judges and lawyers, severely beat Fanning, wrecked his house and terrorized some residents who remained unsympathetic to their cause.

At the next assembly, also in September 1770, Tryon and the delegates intended to consider reforms to help small farmers in the backcountry. But rumors reached them that armed Regulators were marching to New Bern to confront them and possibly riot. Instead of passing reforms, they refused to seat Herman Husband, who had been elected to the assembly, and had him jailed for threatening the assembly and inciting riot. The assembly also passed the Johnston Riot Act, which allowed colonial authorities to move court cases involving riots from one county to another. The act also stipulated that anyone who did not respond to a court summons involving a riot case could be shot on sight as an outlaw, and that the governor could use the militia to subdue rioters. Possibly in exchange for his release from jail, Husband halted the Regulators moving toward New Bern and convinced them to turn back.

That retreat from the capital, however, did not end the Regulators' defiant agitation. They pledged not to pay taxes and to kill Fanning. They threatened judges and clerks of court and vowed not to let the county courts convene. In March 1771, the judges of the superior court at Hillsborough informed the governor that they could not hold court without the protection of the militia. Upon receiving their request that he intervene, Tryon felt compelled to resolve, once and for all, the trouble with the Regulators. He was soon to be transferred to New York, where he became governor of that colony, but he wanted the conflict in the backcountry settled first. So, he called out the militia and led them toward Hillsborough.

On May 13, Tryon and 1,100 militiamen arrived at Alamance Creek, near Hillsborough. Between 2,000 and 3,000 Regulators were already camped nearby. To flank the Regulators in Orange County, another unit of militiamen, commanded by Hugh Waddell, a leader from the French and Indian War, had marched toward Salisbury in Rowan County but had been stopped by Regulators from Mecklenburg County. At Alamance, the Regulators first attempted to negotiate with Tryon. He declined to parlay and demanded that they lay down their arms and disband. They refused, and the Battle of Alamance ensued. Tryon's militia carried the day, soundly defeating the Regulators. According to historian Marjoleine Kars, "Estimates of the dead and wounded vary; possibly as many as 20 Regulators were killed, along with 9 militiamen," and a large number of men were wounded. Many Regulators fled the battlefield or surrendered when the battle was lost.

Tryon ordered the public execution of one of the Regulators who had been taken prisoner in the battle. Beneath a tree with a noose around his neck, the rebel, young James Few, a carpenter, was twice offered a pardon by the governor if he would repent and renew his loyalty to the government.

Governor Tryon confronts the regulators. *State Archives of North Carolina*.

When Few refused both times, he was hanged. Kars writes, "Tryon later blamed his troops, claiming they had demanded such 'immediate justice,' but more likely, the governor and his officers wanted to intimidate the local population as well as those of their own soldiers who sympathized with the Regulators."

Tryon offered pardons to all Regulators who would swear loyalty to the government. Eventually more than six thousand Regulators accepted his offer. Some rejected it and fled over the mountains and out of the colony. The governor declared the Regulators' leaders Herman Husband, William Butler, James Hunter and Rednap Howell to be outlaws and offered a reward of money and land to anyone who could secure them, dead or alive. They, too, took flight rather than be captured or killed. In June 1771, a court of oyer and terminer in Hillsborough tried for treason fourteen Regulators who had been captured in battle. The court acquitted two and sentenced twelve to hang. Of those twelve, six were hanged and six were pardoned by the king on the governor's recommendation. Tryon ordered the militia discharged and soon left for New York. His replacement was Josiah Martin, who was the last colonial governor of North Carolina.

The Battle of Alamance had crushed the Regulator movement. However, the popular disaffection that led to the rebellion did not end with the

Regulators' defeat. It would persist for generations and create discord in North Carolina until the problem of sectional conflict was finally addressed by the state government in 1835.

The Regulator rebellion should not be interpreted as a direct revolt against the British king and Parliament and therefore a prelude to the American Revolution. The Regulator movement was an internal conflict within North Carolina against corrupt local officials and illegal taxes and fees. It was a dispute between the poorer classes in the west and the wealthier and more politically powerful interests in the east that dominated the colonial government. The Regulators' objective was to secure for the folk of western North Carolina local autonomy, political equality and individual rights. Ironically, the same colonial leaders who failed to make those concessions to the yeomanry in the backcountry would soon demand identical rights for themselves from the British government in London. When denied those liberties, they would help launch a shattering revolution that would forever change the relationship of North Carolina and the other colonies with Britain and the rest of the world.

6

PRELUDE TO THE AMERICAN REVOLUTION AND STATEHOOD

*I*t might be said that the seeds of the American Revolution were sown with the British victory in the French and Indian War. Following the Treaty of Paris in 1763, Britain emerged as the largest and wealthiest empire in the world, extending all the way from America to India. In North America, it then controlled all of the continent east of the Mississippi River, including Canada and Florida. In exchange for Spain's support during the war and its loss of Florida, France gave to that ally New Orleans and the Louisiana Territory. Plans by Britain's old nemesis to extend its own presence in North America had vanished with battlefield defeat.

Empires, however, are expensive to maintain and defend, and Britain had incurred considerable debt in the war against France. Thus, the mother country began to demand more revenue from North Carolina and the other colonies to pay off that debt and provide for their own defense. Under the policies instituted by George Grenville, the new chancellor of the exchequer, the British Crown began to tighten and enforce its trade and customs laws to prevent evasion and smuggling. With his urging, Parliament passed the Sugar Act of 1764 as a measure to raise revenue through duties paid on molasses and other items imported into the colonies. Prior to its enactment, duties under the Navigation Acts had been levied to ensure that colonial maritime trade favored Britain. The Sugar Act was different in that its purpose was specifically to raise revenue for the government of Britain, which would be used to govern and defend the colonies. According to the old Molasses Act of 1753, New England rum manufacturers were required to pay a duty on the molasses that they imported to make rum. Many had managed to avoid payment by smuggling or bribing customs officers or simply because customs agents had not been diligent in collecting duties. Now under the Sugar Act of 1764, although the duty per gallon on molasses would be reduced, it would be more assiduously collected. That raised the ire of the New England rum manufacturers, who were accustomed to avoiding payment altogether. Other Americans had some concerns about the Sugar Act's levying a direct tax on them, but they generally acquiesced to the legislation. Protest came mostly from New England. North Carolina raised little objection, because it did not have a large rum industry or import much molasses.

However, the next monetary measure enacted by Grenville and Parliament raised a firestorm of protest throughout all the colonies. In February 1765, Grenville sent to Parliament a bill for legislation called the stamp tax, and it became law the following month. The Stamp Act of 1765 mandated the use of stamps or stamped paper for all sorts of documents and publications, such as deeds, wills, customs papers, newspapers, pamphlets, published notices, almanacs and even playing cards and dice. The stamps verified that the new tax had been paid on those items. Angry protests against the stamp tax rang throughout the colonies. North Carolinians and their colonial neighbors proclaimed it to be "taxation without representation." They maintained that because they were not directly represented in Parliament, that governing body had no right to tax them. Only their local assemblies, in which they had representatives, could tax them, they asserted. Organized resistance to the Stamp Act, led by men known as the Sons of Liberty, ignited in all the colonies. In North Carolina, leaders of the Sons of Liberty were prominent planters, merchants and officials in the Cape Fear counties—men such as Cornelius Harnett, Hugh Waddell and John Ashe. In North Carolina, public demonstrations took place in several towns. But the only violent opposition in the colony occurred in the lower Cape Fear region.

The act was to go into effect on November 1, 1765. In Wilmington, on October 31, a large crowd gathered to protest the hated legislation. When the stamp agent William Houston arrived in the town on November 16, the Sons of Liberty seized him and forced him to resign. Then they joined a large crowd in drinking toasts with "the best liquors to be had." On November 28, the British ship *Diligence* reached Brunswick with a supply of stamps and stamped paper. But those items remained onboard the ship, as local protestors would not allow them to be unloaded. In the meantime, trade had come to a standstill, Governor Tryon had closed the courts and no ships had cleared the port.

Then in January 1766, two merchant ships, the *Dobbs* and the *Patience*, arrived at Brunswick. Because their clearance papers were not stamped, the captain of the British ship *Viper* took possession of the two vessels. In response, the Sons of Liberty broke into the customs office and confiscated the ships' papers. They went aboard the *Viper* and forced the captain to release the two merchant ships. Harnett then led the Sons of Liberty to Governor Tryon's house in Wilmington and demanded that he give up the customs agent William Pennington, who had taken refuge at the governor's residence. Pennington agreed to resign his office and promised the crowd that had gathered in the center of town that he would not issue any stamps in North Carolina.

Surprised and concerned about such responses throughout the colonies to the Stamp Act, Parliament repealed the law in 1766 as an effort at appeasement. At the same time, however, it passed the Declaratory Act, which proclaimed that—despite what Americans insisted—Parliament did indeed have the authority and right to tax the colonies. As if to prove their point, British lawmakers passed the Townshend Acts, which placed duties on wine, tea, paper, glass and lead purchased in the colonies. The taxes were intended to pay the salaries of colonial governors and judges, who had previously been paid by the colonial assemblies. The North Carolina Assembly did not protest the Townshend taxes. Instead, in 1768, it sent an appeal to King George III, asking him to persuade Parliament to revoke the duties. The king ignored the request.

With the Townshend Acts still in effect, considerable opposition to their enforcement arose in New England, especially in the port of Boston, where some merchants attempted to circumvent the duties and frequently engaged in smuggling that led the Royal Navy to confiscate American vessels and cargo. To enforce its authority and laws and to quell any possible violence, the British government landed additional troops in the Massachusetts port in late September 1768. Bostonians became increasingly angry at Parliament's Quartering Act of 1765, which called upon colonists to provide quarters for the troops, even taking them into their homes.

As tensions grew between the mother country and the Americans over the royal government's taxes, Virginia's House of Burgesses called for colonial "nonimportation associations," whereby the colonies would collectively agree not to import any items on which duties had to be paid. When the North Carolina Assembly met in October 1769, Speaker of the House John Harvey proposed approval of the "association." Governor Tryon, however, hearing of that pending action, dissolved the assembly. Harvey then called a "convention" in New Bern, where sixty-four of the seventy-four former members of the assembly met and approved a "nonimportation association."

The quarrel continued to swell between Bostonians' asserting their rights to oppose taxes imposed on them and Parliament's insistence on its authority to levy such duties. The situation finally boiled over in the so-called Boston Massacre on March 5, 1770. Redcoat soldiers fired on a belligerent crowd in front of the customhouse, killing three people and wounding eight. Bostonians exaggerated the "massacre" but nevertheless hardened their opposition to British policies and won the sympathy of the other colonies.

Parliament attempted to reconcile with the colonists over the hated taxes by revoking all the duties on items specified in the Townshend Acts, except tea. Tempers cooled for a time, and importation resumed, although an undercurrent of resistance and suspicion continued to flow. Trouble erupted again in 1772 over the royal government's pending trial of men in Rhode Island who were accused of attacking and burning the revenue schooner *Gaspee*, which had been pursuing smugglers. Massachusetts developed further worries about British policies when Governor Thomas Hutchinson announced that in the future, his salary and those of the colony's judges would come directly from the British Crown. Such a policy broke from the past practice of salaries' being allotted by the colonial legislature and thereby weakened the power the colonists had over their local government. Massachusetts urged the colonies to form "committees of correspondence" to address future actions of the royal government, to stay in touch with each other and to prepare to respond collectively. Led first by Massachusetts and then by Virginia, all the colonies established such committees. North Carolina created its committee in December 1773. The nine members of the committee were Richard Caswell, John Harvey, Robert Howe, Cornelius Harnett, Edward Vail, William Hooper, John Ashe, Joseph Hewes and Samuel Johnston. All were men of wealth and influence. Eight of them came from either the Albemarle or the Cape Fear region. Only Caswell was from the middle part of the coastal plain. His plantations were located near the town of Kingston (renamed Kinston in the American Revolution).

In the same month that North Carolina formed its Committee of Correspondence, the famed Boston Tea Party occurred. It followed the Tea Act of May 1773, which set new policies on collecting the tax on tea. The act ended the duty in England and collected it only in America, and it gave virtual control of the tea trade in the colonies to the East India Company by making it possible for that company to undersell American merchants. When a consignment of East India Company tea arrived in

Boston in December, local protestors demanded that the ships transporting the tea leave the harbor without unloading their cargo. However, Governor Hutchinson ordered that the tea be taken off the vessels before they could leave the harbor. To prevent the unloading, a group of Bostonians ill disguised as Indians boarded the ships and threw the tea into the harbor.

Now angry and out of patience with Boston and Massachusetts as a whole, the government in England concluded that the Bostonians had finally gone too far with their so-called tea party and cracked down on them by passing the Coercive Acts of March–June 1774. The first act closed the port of Boston to trade. The second declared that the king, not the colony's assembly, would appoint the members of the governor's council, and that other officials and judges would be appointed or removed by the governor or nominated by him for the king's approval. It also prohibited the convening of town meetings, except to elect town officials. The third act mandated that any royal official or soldier charged with a capital crime be tried in England or Nova Scotia in order to avoid a biased jury in Massachusetts. The fourth act enforced the quartering of British troops, who would be arriving in greater numbers to protect royal authorities and property and to keep law and order. To enforce the acts, the British government appointed General Thomas Gage, who commanded British troops in North America, as the military governor of Massachusetts.

Although the Coercive Acts, which the colonists called the Intolerable Acts, targeted Boston and Massachusetts in general, the other colonies identified with their plight, realizing that the same restrictions and mandates could be inflicted on them, and they voiced their support for Boston. North Carolina's Committee of Correspondence proclaimed that all the colonies "ought to consider themselves interested in the cause of the town of Boston as the cause of America in general." The members vowed that they would cooperate with any measures agreed to by the committees of the other colonies, and they declared that in order to encourage and achieve "conformity and unanimity in the councils of America…a continental congress was absolutely necessary."

Shortly after Parliament issued the Coercive Acts, Massachusetts urged all the colonies to elect delegates to meet in Philadelphia in September to discuss how to respond to Britain's actions. In North Carolina, Governor Josiah Martin, who had succeeded Tryon in 1771, refused to call the assembly into session in time to elect delegates to a conference in Philadelphia. "In that case," responded Speaker of the House John Harvey, "the people will hold a convention independent of the Governor." Local meetings throughout North

Carolina then elected delegates to North Carolina's First Provincial Congress, which met in New Bern in August. The Provincial Congress, moderated by Harvey, convened for three days, condemned Parliament's tax policies, pledged support for Boston and Massachusetts, agreed to recognize any boycott of trade with Britain and elected delegates to the First Continental Congress, set to meet in Philadelphia. The delegates elected were William Hooper, Joseph Hewes and Richard Caswell.

At the First Continental Congress in Philadelphia in September 1774, North Carolina's delegates voted with the other colonies' representatives for the Suffolk Resolves, originally proposed by Massachusetts. The resolves called for a collective boycott of trade with Britain and opposition to the Coercive Acts. Before it adjourned on October 26, the congress established the Continental Association to guide the prohibition against British trade. It also authorized committees of safety in the counties and towns of the colonies to enforce the trade boycott, begin forming militias and promote and enforce loyalty to the American cause among their local populaces. As time went on, those committees assumed more power as local and civil governments.

While the Continental Congress held its session, conflict between British authorities and the residents of Massachusetts continued to grow, and the other colonies became increasingly sympathetic to the New England colony and defiant in their own relationships with the royal government. In Edenton, North Carolina, in October 1774, fifty-one women, led by Penelope Barker, gathered at the house of Elizabeth King. They signed an agreement to resist to the best of their abilities any injustice leveled against Americans by the king and Parliament, including not purchasing tea or other items imported from Britain. That early political activity by colonial women caught the attention of the press back in London. One magazine published a cartoon of the so-called Edenton Tea Party. The faces of the women portrayed in the drawing were actually the faces of some of Britain's leading politicians, who seemed to be bungling affairs with the colonies.

A disgruntled Governor Martin denounced the Continental Congress, the trade embargo and the committees of safety. He summoned the assembly into session in New Bern on April 4, 1775, in part to address the defiance and dissatisfaction in the colony. At the same time, John Harvey called for North Carolina's Second Provincial Congress to convene in New Bern. Most members of the Provincial Congress were also members of the assembly. Both bodies, then, met at the same time and elected Harvey speaker of the assembly, thereby having him preside over the congress and the legislature

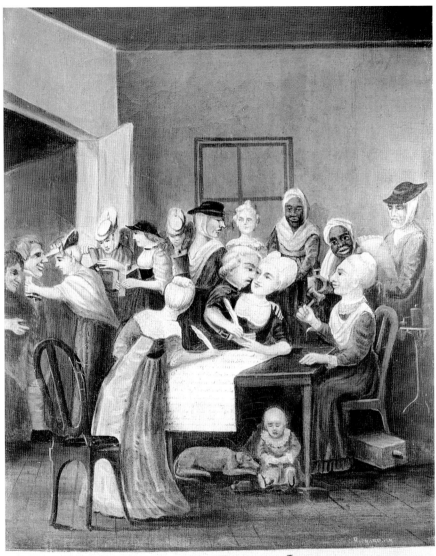

A SOCIETY of PATRIOTIC LADYS.
AT
EDENTON NORTH CAROLINA.

Plate V.

London. Printed for R.Sayer & J.Bennett. No 53 in Fleet Street as the Act directs. 25 March 1775.

The Edenton Tea Party (1774). *State Archives of North Carolina.*

simultaneously. The Provincial Congress approved the actions of the First Continental Congress and asserted the people's rights to assemble and to petition the British Crown about their grievances. It authorized Harvey to call another Provincial Congress if necessary. Annoyed and exasperated, Martin dissolved the assembly, which was the last royal assembly to meet in North Carolina.

Meanwhile, back in Massachusetts, General Gage had received orders to seize any arms and ammunition that might be used by the colonials against British troops. He heard that such munitions were stored at Concord, a town northwest of Boston. On April 18, redcoats marched from Boston with the objective of seizing the weapons and ammunition at Concord and arresting rebel leaders. But local minutemen (volunteer militiamen) had received advance warning by riders, including the famed Paul Revere, that British troops were on their way to Concord. En route, the king's soldiers fired on a contingent of minutemen who had formed on the green in the town of Lexington. They then moved on to Concord, where they found only a small quantity of supplies. As the redcoats marched back to Boston, minutemen constantly attacked their extended columns. By the time they reached the city, 275 British soldiers and 95 minutemen had been killed or wounded. Minutemen and militiamen then surrounded Boston, placing the British under siege. With actual fighting having broken out and Boston besieged, the Second Continental Congress met in Philadelphia on May 10 and instructed the colonies to begin to make preparations for war.

Word of the combat at Lexington and Concord spread throughout the colonies and excited American anger. In North Carolina, committees of safety spurred on efforts to organize and equip local troops, and talk of independence from the mother country rumbled through the population. Those Americans who supported independence came to be known as Whigs or Patriots. But not all the colonials favored a break from Britain. Those who supported the British government and opposed separation were called Loyalists or Tories. Many Loyalists lived in North Carolina, and disruption and violence between them and the Whigs became common. Eventually, a number of them fought with the British.

The Mecklenburg County Committee of Safety was swept with such an anti-British fervor that it passed the Mecklenburg Resolves on May 31, 1775. The resolves stated that Mecklenburg County would not obey British laws and would govern itself until either the Provincial Congress established a permanent government or "the legislative body of Great Britain resign[ed] its unjust and arbitrary pretensions with respects to America."

At the same time that Mecklenburg County was composing its resolves in Charlotte, Governor Josiah Martin fled the capital in New Bern. Reports had reached him that armed Patriots were on their way to take the capital and capture him. He had already sent his family to New York, where they could be protected by British troops. Martin first took refuge at Fort Johnston in the lower Cape Fear region. But hearing that a large force of minutemen was on the march to seize him, he left the fort and boarded the British sloop *Cruizer*. With that departure, he became the last royal governor to rule in North Carolina. In July, Cornelius Harnett, John Ashe and Robert Howe led five hundred minutemen in taking over Fort Johnston and burning it down to prevent its possible use by the British. Although this was a small event, this operation might be considered the first military action against the government of Britain by its former subjects in North Carolina.

In the previous month, however, a major battle had been fought in Massachusetts. The British had continued to reinforce Boston after the Battles of Lexington and Concord, and Massachusetts increased the size of its militia surrounding the city. On June 14, the Second Continental Congress established an army, known as the Continental Line, and appointed George Washington as its commander, with orders to go to the Boston area to take charge of the colonial troops there. But before Washington arrived, a furious battle was fought in the hills overlooking the port city.

On June 17, the British launched an attack from Boston to drive the Americans off Breed's Hill, adjacent to Bunker Hill. In the fighting that followed, which became known as the Battle of Bunker Hill, the redcoats suffered tremendous casualties before securing their objective. Washington reached the Boston area on July 2 and took command of the Continental army. After Washington captured Dorchester Heights in March 1776, the British evacuated Boston and moved their main headquarters to New York.

In Philadelphia, the Continental Congress, recognizing that it had a regular army in the field to confront what was almost certain to be more major fighting, took on the authority and responsibilities of a central government, a role that it held throughout the conflict that lay ahead. It issued paper money to fund the army, established a committee for foreign negotiations and urged the colonies to increase their war preparations. North Carolina's delegates, Hooper, Hewes and Caswell, encouraged the leaders back home to increase their efforts to mobilize the people.

North Carolina's Third Provincial Congress convened in Hillsborough in August 1775, and it carried out the measures called for by the Continental Congress. It raised two regiments to serve in the new Continental army and organized six regiments of six hundred militiamen each from the six military districts. It praised Hooper, Hewes and Caswell for their service at the Continental Congress and reelected them to continue to serve as delegates. Caswell, however, resigned from that position to serve as the treasurer of the Southern District of North Carolina. The Provincial Congress then elected John Penn, a lawyer and farmer in Granville County, to replace Caswell.

At this time, no major fighting had taken place in North Carolina, and none of the colonies had committed to a complete break from the mother country. In fact, they had offered the possibility of reconciliation in a document sent to the king called the Olive Branch Petition. King George III, however, rejected the petition and declared the colonies in rebellion. In the north, more fighting followed the Battles of Lexington and Concord and Bunker Hill. Americans clashed with British troops at Fort Ticonderoga on Lake Champlain in May 1775 and in a failed expedition to Quebec in Canada in December. It would not be long, though, before the fighting moved south, and North Carolina would soon become a major target for the British.

From the safety of the *Cruizer*, Governor Martin helped persuade the British army to send an expedition to the colony. He maintained that North Carolina had a large force of Loyalists who would rally to Britain and fight against the Whigs, or Patriots, in a southern campaign. He anticipated correctly that the largest number of Loyalist combatants would come from the Highland Scots of the Cross Creek area on the Cape Fear. He also believed that some of the Regulators from the backcountry would join in support of a British campaign in the Carolinas. He issued a proclamation to the Loyalists to arm and organize.

Authorities in England, acting in part on the advice of Martin, planned, in early 1776, to have two fleets transport troops to the Cape Fear. Sir Henry Clinton and an army would sail from Boston. Another expedition, commanded by Lord Charles Cornwallis, would leave from Ireland. The Loyalists recruited by Martin would march from Cross Creek toward Brunswick and Wilmington and unite with the British who were coming by water. The combined force would then proceed to attack Charles Town, South Carolina, and capture that vital port.

To organize a Tory army in North Carolina and lead it to the coast, General Gage dispatched 2 officers, General Donald MacDonald and Lieutenant Colonel Donald MacLeod. In response, North Carolina's Whigs called out the militia and one regiment of Continental troops. Colonel James

Moore was in overall command of the Patriots. MacDonald and about 1,600 Tories—mostly Highland Scots, with perhaps 200 former Regulators—set out on a march to Wilmington. Two of Moore's subordinates, Colonels Richard Caswell and Alexander Lillington, and their troops established a defensive position in front of MacDonald's column. The site of the Whigs' position was about seventeen miles north of Wilmington at Moore's Creek Bridge, named for landowner and widow Mary Moore. When the Loyalists attacked on February 17, 1776, they faced the difficulty of crossing the wooden bridge with Caswell's and Lillington's men in position on the other side. The Whigs had removed many of the planks on the bridge. As the Loyalists attempted to cross, they came under devastating fire from volleys of the Whigs' muskets and two artillery pieces named "Old Mother Covington and her daughter."

The battle lasted only minutes. At least thirty of the Tories were killed outright, and more died later of their wounds. Only two of Caswell's and Lillington's men were wounded, though one later died from his injury. The Whigs captured many of the Loyalists who attempted to flee. About 850 of the rank-and-file soldiers who surrendered received paroles. However, their officers, of whom there were about 30, were jailed at Halifax. General MacDonald was among those imprisoned. The paroled Loyalists who returned to their communities often clashed, sometimes violently, with their Patriot neighbors. Some had their property confiscated after a state government was formed, and a number fled to Nova Scotia or other parts of Canada. The conflict between Whigs and Tories, referred to as the Tory War, at times became an inner civil war in North Carolina and continued until the end of the American Revolution. A number of Loyalists joined and fought in British regiments as the war unfolded in the Carolinas.

The Battle of Moore's Creek Bridge might have turned out differently if the troops of Clinton and Cornwallis had arrived on time to rendezvous with the Loyalists. But their two fleets did not assemble at Cape Fear until May 3, 1776. Some landing parties came ashore and raided and plundered along the Cape Fear River, but the raids achieved no tactical benefit. The fleets soon weighed anchor and moved on to attack Charles Town in South Carolina. The British failed to capture that port, and North Carolina militia helped repulse their assault.

The Battle of Moore's Creek Bridge had been the first major clash of arms in North Carolina. The Whig victory against the Tories and the subsequent failure to take Charles Town had denied the British a foothold in the southern colonies. There would be no invasion of North Carolina until 1780, when the redcoats returned to the Carolinas. But blood had been shed in North Carolina and, along with it, any hopes of reconciliation with Britain.

When delegates gathered at North Carolina's Fourth Provincial Congress in Halifax in April 1776, a cry for independence was almost certain to be the result. On April 12, the congress approved the Halifax Resolves, North Carolina's first official commitment to separation from the mother country. The resolves instructed the colony's delegates to the Continental Congress to vote along with the representatives from the other colonies for independence from Britain. The Provincial Congresses of the other colonies also had instructed their delegates to vote for independence, and all were now joined in a united effort. The Continental Congress urged the colonies to create independent governments, and it formed a committee to establish a confederation of all the colonies. New Hampshire, South Carolina and Virginia quickly began writing constitutions, and others would follow suit. North Carolina's Fourth Provincial Congress considered drafting a temporary constitution as a basis for a central government, but it decided to postpone such a document. Instead, it created the North Carolina Council of Safety to act as a central government until a constitution for an independent North Carolina could be drafted. The Council of Safety replaced the Provincial Council, which had been established by the Third Provincial Congress.

At the Continental Congress on June 7, 1776, Richard Henry Lee of Virginia declared "that these United Colonies are and of right ought to be free and independent States." The congress adopted his resolution on July 2 and, two days later, approved the Declaration of Independence, written largely by Thomas Jefferson. The delegates from North Carolina who signed the declaration were William Hooper, Joseph Hewes and John Penn.

Word of the "immortal document" reached the North Carolina Council of Safety, which met in Halifax on July 22. The council quickly passed a resolution that Americans "were absolved from all allegiance to the British Crown." The next task was to write a constitution for the newly declared independent state of North Carolina, specifying the structure and nature of its government and the rights of the people under its jurisdiction. On August 9, the Council of Safety called for an election to be held on October 12 for the voters to choose delegates to a Fifth Provincial Congress, which was to convene at Halifax for the purpose of drafting North Carolina's first state constitution. The council urged the voters "to pay close attention" in selecting their delegates, because those representatives were "to form a Constitution for this State," which would be "the Corner Stone of all Laws, so it ought to be fixed and Permanent and promote the happiness or Misery of the State."

The Fifth Provincial Congress met in Halifax on November 12, 1776, and devoted considerable hours to discussing a state constitution and a bill of rights. Richard Caswell presided as both president of the congress and chairman of the committee that drafted the documents. The delegates first approved the bill, called the Declaration of Rights, on November 17, and the constitution on the following day. The two were then printed and distributed throughout North Carolina, but they were not presented to the voters for popular ratification. The Declaration of Rights contained twenty-five articles that specified North Carolinians' individual rights. The North Carolina Constitution created three branches of state government: executive, legislative and judicial. The document deliberately limited the authority of the governor, placing the greatest political power in the General Assembly. That legislature would elect the governor and appoint all members of the executive branch and the judges. Governors could serve one-year terms and could serve only three terms in a six-year period. The Council of State had to approve all actions taken by a governor. Those measures were an attempt to avoid in the new state government some of the difficulties that North Carolina had previously had with its colonial governors. The constitution also set some property qualifications for voting and holding state offices. Only adult males could vote. The Provincial Congress appointed Richard Caswell as interim governor, until the General Assembly could meet in January 1777 and officially elect him the first governor of the state of North Carolina.

In declaring its independence from Britain and establishing its own constitution and government, North Carolina was severing its ties to its colonial past. But declaring independence and actually winning it on the battlefield against the world's greatest military power were two different situations. A long war lay ahead for North Carolina and the other twelve states before their independence would finally be secured after a bloody struggle that raged throughout the former colonies.

During the Revolutionary War, North Carolinians fought in both the northern and southern campaigns. About 10,000 served in the militia, and between 6,086 and 7,663 served in the Continental army. At various times, 1,500 militiamen were assigned to the Continental army. North Carolina's Continental troops joined George Washington's army in the north, participated in operations at the Battle of Brandywine and sustained major casualties at the Battle of Germantown in Pennsylvania in the fall of

1777. They were with Washington during the hard winter of 1777–78 at Valley Forge and fought in the Battle of Monmouth in New Jersey in late June 1778.

Back in North Carolina, the Cherokee, led by Chief Attakullakulla, or "Little Carpenter," allied with the British and attacked western White settlements in the spring of 1776. In retaliation, North Carolina, South Carolina, Georgia and Virginia combined forces to defeat the Cherokee. General Griffith Rutherford commanded the North Carolina militia in the campaign. His men destroyed numerous towns of the Cherokee, ruined their crops and killed and scalped many of them. Overwhelmed, the Cherokee signed a peace treaty in July 1777, giving up all claims to lands east of the Blue Ridge Mountains.

Unable to force a surrender of Washington's army in the northern theater, the British turned once again to the south in 1778. A force led by Sir Henry Clinton captured the Georgia port of Savannah on July 29. North Carolina's General Robert Howe, commanding the Southern Department of the Continental Line, received the blame for the defeat and was court-martialed, although he remained in the American army. Clinton's army next captured Charles Town, South Carolina, with an overwhelming victory in May 1780. Two brigades of Continental troops from North Carolina and six hundred of its militiamen took part in the battle. General Benjamin Lincoln, who had succeeded Howe, led the Americans in the defeat and was removed from command of the Department of the South. With Charles Town secured, the British, under General Cornwallis, were posed to march north through South Carolina and into North Carolina.

The North Carolina militia, commanded by former governor Richard Caswell, mobilized with Continental soldiers under the leadership of General Horatio Gates, who had replaced Lincoln, to halt the British advance. But in August 1780, Cornwallis's men routed the Americans at the Battle of Camden, South Carolina, killing eight hundred Patriots and capturing one thousand. Approximately half of the dead were North Carolinians. Gates, Caswell and the remnants of their forces fled back into North Carolina. The defeat at Camden left North Carolina open to invasion.

Cornwallis then set his army on a march to Charlotte, North Carolina, where he hoped to occupy the town and recruit Loyalist volunteers. However, constant harassment by Patriot partisans hindered his operations and cut off contact with the Tories. He experienced a further setback when Colonel Patrick Ferguson, whom he had sent to protect his left flank with a force of British regulars and Loyalists, was crushed by the North Carolina militia and a group known as the Over-Mountain Men at the Battle of Kings Mountain on October 7, 1780. The battle took place in South Carolina, just over the southern border of North Carolina's Cleveland County. That loss forced Cornwallis to retreat back into South Carolina to regroup.

American fortunes improved further when General Nathanael Greene became the new commander of the Southern Department in early December 1780. On January 17, 1781, his subordinate Colonel Daniel Morgan, with one thousand men, of whom three hundred were North Carolinians, won a decisive victory over Colonel Banastre Tarleton at the Battle of Cowpens, South Carolina. Greene then began to pull the two separate wings of his army back into North Carolina with the intention of having Cornwallis chase him, thus drawing the British farther away from their supply lines and depleting their ranks. That tactic worked. As Cornwallis pursued the Patriots, his men suffered from the harsh winter weather and a shortage of supplies. Swollen rivers hindered their progress, and they burned much of their baggage in order to move with more speed. Meanwhile, Greene had managed to stay ahead of Cornwallis, withdrawing north across the Virginia border, increasing the size of his army to four thousand and uniting its two wings. He then prepared to do battle with Cornwallis, who was 230 miles from a supply center with a depleted force. The British had halted at Hillsborough.

The two armies finally engaged in a vicious fight at the Battle of Guilford Courthouse in Guilford County on March 15, 1781. North Carolina militiamen stood in the first two lines, opposing the British assault and sustaining a large number of casualties. The redcoats, however, suffered the most killed and wounded, which considerably weakened their ranks. Greene withdrew from the battlefield in order to continue attacks on British outposts at Camden and Ninety-Six, South Carolina, and Augusta, Georgia. Greene's withdrawal from the Guilford battlefield led Cornwallis to declare himself the victor. But his army was so depleted that he had to march to Wilmington, which was then occupied by a British garrison, to recuperate and resupply. Unable to confront and destroy Greene's army, Cornwallis decided to leave Wilmington, march into Virginia and unite with other British troops who had invaded that state.

In August 1781, Cornwallis entrenched his troops in fortifications at Yorktown, Virginia. Meanwhile, in North Carolina, the Tory War, led primarily by the notorious Loyalist David Fanning, continued to wreak havoc in some areas. Cornwallis's decision to encamp his army at Yorktown proved to be his downfall. There, he was encircled and trapped by Washington's army and a large allied French army and naval expedition and compelled to surrender on October 19, 1781.

The surrender by Cornwallis at Yorktown technically concluded the Revolutionary War. The government of Britain, tired of a long, exhausting war that it could not seem to win, no longer wanted to continue the expensive struggle to retain its American colonies. The British would occupy the cities of New York, Charleston (Charles Town) and Savannah until the Treaty of Paris of 1783 officially ended the conflict and the United States embarked on its own course. No longer a colony subservient to its mother country, North Carolina now assumed the status and challenges of statehood in a new democratic nation soon to emerge as a world power.

BIBLIOGRAPHY

Bailyn, Bernard, et al. *The Great Republic: A History of the American People*. Lexington, MA: D.C. Heath, 1977.

Blethen, H. Tyler, and Curtis W. Wood Jr. *From Ulster to Carolina: The Migration of the Scotch-Irish to Southwestern North Carolina*. 2nd rev. ed. Raleigh: North Carolina Office of Archives and History, 1998.

Butler, Lindley S. *Pirates, Privateers, and Rebel Raiders of the North Carolina Coast*. Chapel Hill: University of North Carolina Press, 2000.

Butler, Lindley S., and Alan D. Watson, eds. *The North Carolina Experience: An Interpretive and Documentary History*. Chapel Hill: University of North Carolina Press, 1984.

Byrd, William. *William Byrd's Histories of the Dividing Line betwixt Virginia and North Carolina*. Edited by William K. Boyd. New York: Dover Publications, 1967.

Crow, Jeffrey J. *A Chronicle of North Carolina during the American Revolution, 1763–1789*. 2nd printing. Raleigh: North Carolina Office of Archives and History, 1997.

Crow, Jeffrey J., Paul D. Escott and Flora J. Hatley Wadelington. *A History of African Americans in North Carolina*. 2nd rev. ed. Raleigh: North Carolina Office of Archives and History, 2011.

Ekirch, A. Roger. *"Poor Carolina": Politics and Society in Colonial North Carolina, 1729–1776*. Chapel Hill: University of North Carolina Press, 1981.

Fenn, Elizabeth A., Peter Wood, et al. *The Way We Lived in North Carolina*. Edited by Joe A. Mobley. Chapel Hill: University of North Carolina Press, 2003.

Kars, Marjoleine. *Breaking Loose Together: The Regulator Rebellion in Pre-Revolutionary North Carolina*. Chapel Hill: University of North Carolina Press, 2002.

Lawson, John. *A New Voyage to Carolina*. Edited by Hugh Talmage Lefler. Chapel Hill: University of North Carolina Press, 1967.

Lefler, Hugh Talmage, and Albert Ray Newsome. *North Carolina: The History of a Southern State*. Chapel Hill: University of North Carolina Press, 1973.

Lefler, Hugh Talmage, and William S. Powell. *Colonial North Carolina: A History*. New York: Charles Scribner's Sons, 1973.

Merrens, H. Roy. *Colonial North Carolina in the Eighteenth Century: A Study in Historical Geography*. Chapel Hill: University of North Carolina Press, 1964.

Parker, Mattie Erma Edwards, ed. *North Carolina Charters and Constitutions, 1578–1698*. Vol. 1. *The Colonial Records of North Carolina* (Second Series). Raleigh, NC: Carolina Charter Tercentenary Commission, 1963.

Perdue, Theda, and Christopher Arris Oakley. *Native Carolinians: The Indians of North Carolina*. Raleigh: North Carolina Office of Archives and History, 2010.

Powell, William S. *North Carolina through Four Centuries*. Chapel Hill: University of North Carolina Press, 1989.

Powell, William S., ed. *The Correspondence of William Tryon and Other Selected Papers, 1758–1818*. 2 vols. Raleigh: North Carolina Office of Archives and History, 1980–1981.

———. *Dictionary of North Carolina Biography*. 6 vols. Chapel Hill: University of North Carolina Press, 1979–1996.

———. *Encyclopedia of North Carolina*. Chapel Hill: University of North Carolina Press, 2006.

Powell, William S., and Michael Hill. *The North Carolina Gazetteer: A Dictionary of Tar Heel Places and Their History*. 2nd rev. ed. Chapel Hill: University of North Carolina Press, 2010.

Quinn, David B., and Alison M. Quinn, eds. *The First Colonists: Documents on the Planting of the First English Settlements in North America*. 2nd printing. Raleigh: North Carolina Office of Archives and History, 1985.

Ready, Milton. *The Tar Heel State: A History of North Carolina*. Columbia: University of South Carolina Press, 2003.

Saunders, William L., ed. *The Colonial Records of North Carolina*. 10 vols. Raleigh: State of North Carolina, 1886–1890.

Schaw, Janet. *Journal of a Lady of Quality*. Edited by Evangeline W. Andrews and Charles M. Andrews. New Haven, CT: Yale University Press, 1921.

Smith, Margaret Supplee, and Emily Herring Wilson. *North Carolina Women Making History*. Chapel Hill: University of North Carolina Press, 1999.

Stick, David. *Roanoke Island: The Beginnings of English America*. Chapel Hill: University of North Carolina Press, 2002.

Troxler, Carole Watterson. *Farming Dissenters: The Regulator Movement in Piedmont North Carolina*. Raleigh: North Carolina Office of Archives and History, 2011.

Watson, Alan D. *Society in Colonial North Carolina*. 2nd rev. ed. Raleigh: North Carolina Office of Archives and History, 2002.

Watson, Alan D., ed. *Society in Early North Carolina: A Documentary History*. Raleigh: North Carolina Office of Archives and History, 2010.

Wood, Bradford J. "A Colony Lost: North Carolina in Atlantic World Histories." *North Carolina Historical Review* 98 (April 2021): 123–51.

INDEX

ABOUT THE AUTHOR

*J*oe A. Mobley taught history at North Carolina State University after retiring from the North Carolina Office of Archives and History. He has authored a number of articles and twelve books, received a North Caroliniana Book Award for the best book on North Carolina and served as president of both the North Carolina Literary and Historical Association and the Historical Society of North Carolina. His other titles for The History Press include *Raleigh: A Brief History*; *Confederate Generals of North Carolina: Tar Heels in Command*; and *North Carolina Governor Richard Caswell: Founding Father and Revolutionary Hero*.

Visit us at
www.historypress.com